LAUGH FOR GOD'S SAKE
Where Jewish Humor and Jewish Ethics Meet

LAUGH FOR GOD'S SAKE

Where Jewish Humor and Jewish Ethics Meet

STANLEY J. SCHACHTER

KTAV Publishing House, Inc.

Jersey City, NJ

Library of Congress Cataloging-in-Publication Data

Schachter, Stanley J.
  Laugh for God's sake : where Jewish humor and Jewish ethics meet / Stanley
J. Schachter.
     p. cm.
   ISBN 978-1-60280-018-2
 . 1. Jewish wit and humor--History and criticism. 2. Jews--Humor. 3.
Business--Humor. 4. Jewish ethics. I. Title.
   PN6149.J4S33 2008
   808.88'2089924--dc22

                              2008001487

    3 1967 01058 3048

                          Published by
              KTAV Publishing House, Inc.
                     930 Newark Avenue
                   Jersey City, NJ 07306
                 Email: bernie@ktav.com
                       www.ktav.com
                      (201) 963-9524
                     Fax (201) 963-0102

TO LIFSA

(Proverbs 31:29)

TABLE OF CONTENTS

PREFACE

The biblical writer Ecclesiastes (Kohelet) observed that "of the making of many books, there is no limit." We may paraphrase his somewhat off-putting words by observing that there is hardly a limit to new books on Jewish humor. Nor is this a new phenomenon. It was true during the past century when secular Yiddish writing was in its heyday. It is true in Israel where Hebrew has succeeded Yiddish as the language of Jewish humor.

In America too we can count on the appearance of works of Jewish humor virtually every year, some even achieving the status of best sellers. Jewish humor has burst the confines of Jewish neighborhoods, and these days can even be found comfortably at home in many universities where it has acquired academic stature as an honored and respected branch of folklore studies.

Studies examine Jewish jokes for what they can reveal from the perspective of psychology, sociology, politics and history. Comparative works examine the similarities and differences between Jewish humor and other genres of ethnic humor. Many recent writings serve as literary maps of Jewish responses to anti-Semitism, the Holocaust, immigration to western lands, problems of modernity, Diaspora Jewish minority status, and Israeli Jewish majority status.

The more popular works on Jewish humor are simply anthologies with little or no attempt at analysis. Some use jokes as take-off points for an extended comment on a familiar circumstance in which Jews might find themselves. Only here and there among these works have I seen passing reference to a significant connection between Jewish jokes and distinctive Jewish spiritual values. The purpose of this book is to explore that connection.

One reason for humor's irresistible attraction is that it is never anyone's private property. It is always and quintessentially part of the public domain of a specific culture or folk tradition, passed from one generation to the next through oral transmission. Every joke conceals the identity of the person who first told it as well as its subsequent transmitters, each of whom added a nuance or modification, reshaping and transforming the joke until it reaches us in its most current form. We in our turn will be certain to 'improve' it once again. Currently, the internet has created a new kind of life-after-death, and many once-buried jokes have undergone resurrection. Clad in garb suited to newer times, they are once again providing joy and laughter. This ability of jokes merits the same awe and honor we pay to works of literature that experience new life and become beloved by a new generation of readers.

Jewish humor, like the humor of all other peoples and cultures, is the creation and legacy of the people that created it. The Jewish people are its collective owners. Interpreters of Jewish humor may lay claim to special insights into Jewish jokes, but not to the jokes themselves.

INTRODUCTION

—◇◇—

WHAT JOKES TELL US

JOKES IN GENERAL – JEWISH JOKES IN PARTICULAR

I readily admit that I like a good joke, but I can confess to being even more excited by a good Jewish joke. My parents steeped me in Yiddish and seemed always able to fit a bit of Jewish humor to almost any occasion. Of course, many Jewish jokes, like the jokes of other peoples, create excitement and anticipation by building tension and by an effective punch line that dissolves the tension. As an adult, I began to ask why we Jews tell the kinds of jokes we tell. I wondered whether a connection might exist between Jewish jokes and our Jewish religious teachings. Might Jewish jokes also have an additional purpose, to subtly remind us of basic Jewish ethical concerns? I have found that by looking at Jewish jokes in this way, another message may emerge, more significant and more lasting than what evoked our initial laughter.

My appreciation for the deeper meanings of Jewish humor was sharpened by Sigmund Freud's book, "*Jokes and Their Relation to the Unconscious*" (1905). One of his major conclusions is that jokes "make possible the satisfaction of an instinct – whether lustful or violent – in the face of an obstacle that stands in its way." That obstacle, for Freud, is his famous 'censor,' an internal armed guard who prevents us from giving in to our hostile or lustful impulses. Because we are denied satisfaction of these impulses, we live in a state of tension and frustration, forever seeking to outwit the ever-vigilant guard. Freud's brilliant insight was to show how humor serves as an escape hatch allowing us to express our repressed urges through jokes. Instead of raping and pillaging, we choose a joke as a weapon, releasing our demons by mocking, demeaning, and insulting, through humor.

My intention in this study of Jewish humor is to build on this insight, albeit in ways that are removed from Freud's purpose. I believe that parallel to the censor who frustrates violent and lustful behavior, there is another censor who similarly alerts us when we should be performing virtuous deeds, but aren't. Jewish teachers have long spoken of an innate force in every human being which they named the "*yetzer hara*," that impels us to do evil, but also inhibits us when we wish to do good. They also posited an opposite force, the "*yetzer tov*," that impels us to do good deeds and restrains us from harmful acts. Within us, the two "*yetzers*" are locked in a struggle between what we ought to do and what we actually do. My intention is to show that a significant portion of Jewish humor highlights this struggle. By looking at Jewish jokes in this way, we can find them illuminating Jewish ethical values.

One example: Jews in Poland once enjoyed an economic perk. They were permitted to operate inns and to sell liquor. One story tells of a Jewish innkeeper and his wife who were roused from their sleep on a bitter-cold winter night by loud banging and heart-rending shouts, "Help me! Save me! I'm freezing to death!" The startled innkeeper began to groan, "Oh, the poor man, out on such a terrible night. My heart goes out to him." His wife berated him, "Don't just sit there and feel sorry for him. Do something." The innkeeper replied, "Yes, I'll open the door and I'll bring him in. I'll warm him by the stove. I'll save his life – and I'll lose all my pity for him!"

This joke builds on the tension between the ideal and the real. It traces to a fundamental Jewish religious teaching known as "*hahnassat orhim*," literally, bringing in guests. It originates in the biblical tale of Abraham welcoming three strangers. This simple story became the basis for a highly developed system of obligatory acts of kindness to travelers and strangers in which *hahnassat orhim* operated both formally and informally. It was a badge of honor for any Jewish community to provide temporary lodging for wayfarers in need, a tradition that proudly continues to the present day. Informally, every synagogue was a clearing-house where transient or indigent Jews were matched with householders who hosted them for meals and lodging and the warmth of a shared Sabbath or Festival environment. *Hahnassat orhim* was a religious and social act of both personal and communal responsibility. The innkeeper story is a uniquely Jewish joke in which we see a person caught between what he knows he must do to satisfy his Jewish conscience and what he would rather do. The joke builds on the tension in the story, the contest between the ideal and the real. The punch line offers an absurd dissolution of the inner struggle. But there is a left-over message. This is a joke that wants us to reflect. Its deeper purpose challenges us to ask how much of the innkeeper we see in ourselves, sympathetic, but only from a distance.

Bringing in guests, providing for the stranger, is one of the enduring standards by which Jewish ethical teachings measure us. The innkeeper joke and many other examples of classical Jewish humor are a form of Jewish teaching, articulating Jewish ideals and presenting a prescription for behavior. We hope to show that looking at Jewish humor in this way is a form of *talmud torah*, a valid way of teaching and learning how to relate to our fellow human beings at a higher level.

THE STRUCTURE OF THE BOOK

The jokes selected for this book evoke the tension between ethical ideals and human behavior. It is structured thematically with each chapter devoted to a specific Jewish ethical or spiritual value. Each chapter begins with an over-view of a value, placing it within its religious and historical context. Two humor anecdotes highlight the dissonance that results when, innocently or willfully, we disobey the ethical/spiritual demand. In turn, these anecdotes serve as the text for analysis and commentary tying the jokes back to the main points of the opening essay. Each chapter concludes with an anthology, without commentary, of other jokes of the same category. Hopefully, they will stimulate your own analysis and insights. The reward will be that you will discover what I have discovered, that humor can have multiple meanings and can lead to worthwhile reflections about ethical behavior. Like classical Midrash, which boasted of extracting a minimum of seventy meanings from each line of the Torah, Jewish jokes too carry a rich load of implications, all of them weighty. As Oscar Wilde once said, "If nothing is serious, nothing is funny." I invite you to join in the search for the serious in the funny.

A NOTE ON PRONUNCIATION

Hebrew and Yiddish words in transliteration are generally easy to pronounce, with the single exception of a guttural sound natural to both languages, but totally missing from contemporary English. Throughout this book, we have adopted the simple device of placing a bar under the letter H̲ (upper case) and h̲ (lower case) to indicate this sound. It is the sound we instinctively make when we try to dislodge a fishbone stuck in our throats. It is not necessary to use a fish bone while practicing.

THE DARK SIDE OF MONEY

For the "haves" of society, money is an intoxicating spice. Buying and selling, lending and borrowing, savoring the uses of money to accumulate pleasures of every kind, take up a major share of their time and attention. For life's "have nots," the situation is drastically different. The amassing, protection and wide uses of capital are of little consequence to those whose fundamental need is to be able to put food on the table. By the simple fact of being chronically in need, the poor of our communities constitute an ethical challenge. Their very existence compels us to consider whether and to what extent a society is obligated to help its needy members.

The Jewish answer to this challenge has always been emphatic, proclaiming that no community may close its eyes or its hands to the plight of its poor. Jewish ethical teachings do not budge on this point, insisting that even when the community assists from communal funds, no individual may avoid personal participation in helping the poor. Remarkably, in Jewish teachings, the obligation to give extends even to those who are the recipients of charity. They too are required to set aside a sum, no matter how tiny, for those who are even less fortunate.

The Torah's rules of charity contain a novel feature. Lending money to the poor, provided that the loan is free of interest charges, is considered an act of charity. This may even strike us as being in conflict with the very idea of charity. It must seem strange that the recipient of the loan has been saddled with the burden of repayment. In what way does a loan qualify as charity? How does it promote and advance the ideal of a generous, giving society if a donor has the option of lending rather than outright giving?

One possible answer is that the law speaks from the persistent reality that there are always people who are in no position to give away money. In the Torah's view, they are not exempt from the requirement to perform acts of charity. They may therefore meet their obligation through a loan. Perhaps too, the Torah is shrewdly aware of how painful it is for some people, even those who are favored with surplus means, to part with their money. Providing the alternative of an interest free loan might make available assistance which would otherwise not be forthcoming.

Rabbinic law differentiates loans for commercial needs from loans to alleviate the misery of the poor, permitting interest charges to the former alone. The Torah's term for interest is *nesheh*, literally a bite, the kind that a ferocious beast inflicts upon its prey. Jewish religious law understood interest charges on loans to the poor as yet another affliction. By forgoing interest on this kind of loan, the lender relieves the recipient of an additional financial burden, and thus it may be considered an act of charity.

Regardless of the chosen instrument of charity, whether by outright giving, by loan, or by any creative means we may devise, the underlying ideology of Judaism's social concerns is that a society does not rise to the level of a good society until it becomes an obligated society.

This ideal was often tested under the grim circumstances of people in dire need. Jewish humor does not spare the tension between society's haves and have-nots. It takes us into a realm where money is needed for bread, simply to sustain life. It is a witness to the eternal contest that unfolds when the poor must appeal to the conscience of the rich, not knowing whether the answer will be "yes" or "no." It is here where we meet the contrast between empathy and indifference. We set the stage with two jokes.

> *A beggar Jew wandered from village to village searching for a person who would take pity on him. He stumbled into a village where he was overcome by the delicious aroma of freshly cooked food coming from an open window. He knocked at the door hoping for a bite to eat. A woman opened the door and demanded to know what he wished. "Please," he said, "I'm a poor man. I haven't had a decent meal for days. I beg you to please help me." She replied, "Would you eat some cold soup?" Eagerly, he answered, "Yes!" "In that case," she said, "come back tomorrow; the soup is still hot!"*

⚬⌇⌇⚬

> *Two strangers meet in the market. One says to the other, "Lend me a hundred rubles." The other responds, "One hundred*

rubles? I don't even know you." The first one sighs and says, "People never fail to amaze me. Here no one will lend me money because no one knows me. In my home town, no one will lend me money because they do know me."

〜〜〜〜

What is the common denominator linking these two jokes? It is the lop-sided relationship between the person in need of help and the one who can as easily help or not. We can imagine the unsympathetic housewife chuckling at her verbal cleverness. We can picture her pleasure as she repeats the story to a friend. Meanwhile, the hungry beggar remains as he was; for him nothing has changed. He must continue his search for someone else who may or may not help him.

The second story presents the plight of the poor less starkly but with the important insight that there is at bottom no advantage to being either known or unknown. Nor does the nature of the need matter at all. This joke leads us to the somber conclusion that an appeal for help can as easily fall on deaf ears as on receptive ears.

Both jokes have in common the unevenness of the playing field in the encounter between the haves and the have-nots. This is a given that never changes. The goal of *tzedakah* as a central pillar of Jewish ethics is to make irrelevant whether or not we know anything about the person in need. Hunger is hunger, misery is never less than misery, and it is of no account that the hungry, suffering person may be too lazy to seek or hold a job. Neither defects of personality nor harmful life habits should be allowed to obscure the fact that he is hungry or in pain. Seen in this light, the task is always to look to the person and not to the outer appearance.

MORE STORIES ABOUT JEWS IN NEED

Following the funeral service, the rich man's coffin was slowly escorted to the cemetery. During his lifetime, the deceased was known for his indifference to the poor. A line of relatives followed behind the coffin, their faces lined with sorrow. Suddenly a bedraggled beggar, dressed in rags, joined their ranks and wept bitterly as he walked. One of them asked him, "Why are you weeping? He was no relative of yours." The beggar replied, "That's why I'm weeping."

⸻≈⸻

A wealthy skinflint died. His son did not shed a tear. During the procession to the cemetery, beggars lined the route, rattling their charity boxes. The son suddenly burst into sobs. He was asked," What made you cry now and not earlier?' He answered, "Now I know for certain that my father is dead. Charity boxes are rattling and he isn't running away."

⸻≈⸻

A poor man stood before a rich man and told him that they had been children together in the same town. The rich man looked at him and said contemptuously, "You are mistaken. I have never seen you before, and I have no intention of helping you." The poor man pointed a finger at the rich man and shouted, "Tomorrow you will be a dead man." The rich man was suddenly frightened. In truth, he did know who the poor man was. They had been playmates in childhood. "I apologize," he said, "I do remember you now. I will help you, but first you must tell me what you meant when you said that tomorrow I will be dead. Were you threatening me with harm?" "Oh no," the poor man replied, "but do you remember that I had a brother?" "Of course, I remember him well," said the rich man. The poor man continued, "My brother is no longer alive, but on the day before he died, he also didn't know who I was."

⸻≈⸻

Two volunteers came to a wealthy man to request his support for several indigent Jews. Knowing his ungenerous nature, they expected to be turned away or, at best, to be dismissed with a pittance. To their surprise and pleasure he told them that he would make a substantial gift. He promptly wrote out a check and handed it to them. They thanked him profusely and left, congratulating themselves on their success. An hour later the two solicitors were back at the rich man's home. Apologetically, they said to him, "We are grateful to you for your wonderful contribution, but you neglected to sign the check." The rich man waved his hand at them, "I certainly did not forget to sign my name. I believe in anonymous giving."

⎯⎯ᨆᨆ⎯⎯

The trustees of the community Passover Relief Fund called on a householder to ask for his generous support. He declined, saying, "I am not contributing to the fund because I have a poor brother who needs my help for the holiday." The next day the brother appeared before the trustees and requested assistance for the holiday. They turned to him in puzzlement, "We cannot help you because your brother is already assisting you." The poor man groaned, "It's true that he's my brother, but he doesn't give me one red cent!" The trustees paid a second visit to the wealthy brother and said to him, "You deceived us. You have neither helped your brother or any other poor soul with their holiday needs." The selfish man responded in a haughty voice, "I certainly did not deceive you. All that I told you is that I have a poor brother. I did not say that I have given him something. Surely, if I don't help my own flesh and blood, you can't expect me to give to complete strangers!"

⎯⎯ᨆᨆ⎯⎯

A poor man sought out a prosperous relative in order to ask for a job. The relative inquired, "Are you acquainted with bookkeeping?" "No," came the reply. "Then please tell me what you are able to do," the rich relative asked. The poor relation replied, "I'm good at giving advice." The rich man thought for a moment and declared, "Here are ten rubles. Please advise me what is the quickest way I can get rid of you."

~~~

A notoriously stingy man of means died. In heaven a committee of angels examined his life's record and could not find a single act of charity. Immediately they seized him and began pushing him towards Hell. He protested furiously and screamed at them, "You are making a terrible mistake. I belong in heaven. Forty years ago I performed a great act of charity. I saved a starving man from death. I gave him a penny to buy a slice of bread." Again the angels searched their records and discovered that it was true. With a great flutter of their wings they flew to God's throne and asked the Holy One, "What shall be the correct verdict for this man?" God summoned His heavenly tribunal and deliberated with them. Their decision was unanimous, "Give him back his penny and let him go to Hell."

WORKERS AND BOSSES

The Jewish ethical tradition looks to the Bible for its inspiration, and sees in the Torah's creation saga the source of its attitude towards work. God labored for six days to create the world, and God fashioned human beings in His image (Genesis 1:1). It's a tight, bare bones way of saying that what's good enough for God should be good enough for us. If work, any kind of work, is not beneath the dignity of God, we who are made in God's likeness should never consider work beneath our dignity. The interpreters of Judaism always viewed work in the most positive light, as both a blessing and an obligation. Jewish sages over the centuries were exemplars of their own teachings. The most renowned teachers of Judaism included sandal makers, cloth dyers, field-laborers, black-smiths, and ordinary day laborers. The skilled and the unskilled among them shared the same status, and an employer did not automatically stand on a higher pedestal than an employee. Ancient tales tell of acclaimed Torah teachers who provided for their families by performing the most menial tasks, demonstrating that what counts are honest, conscientious labor by the worker and respectful consideration by the employer.

The Jewish understanding of labor has a long history. We are taught that fathers were duty bound to teach a craft to their sons (BT Kiddushin 29a). A Mishnah sadly observes that idleness and indolence often lead to sin (Avot 2:2). We tend to think that laws benefiting workers are the hall-mark of modern, enlightened societies, yet Talmudic legislation, almost two thousand years ago, established standards governing minimum pay, safety requirements, collective bargaining and health safeguards. Where varying rates of pay for identical work prevailed in the same community, a worker could insist that he be paid at the average rate, not at the lowest one (BT Baba Metzia 87a). If local custom included meals and lodging as part of a pay package, employers were forbidden to deny these perks to their workers (Mishnah, Baba Metzia 7:1). During the many centuries when farm labor was the predominant form of work, field hands were granted the right to eat of the farm produce while working in the fields, but employers were forbidden to pay their workers in kind as a portion of their wages (ibid. 10:5). As a general rule, workers were hired by the day and were to be paid at the end of each day's work. An employer deliberately delaying payment faced public scorning by being declared a robber (BT Baba Metzia 11a). In all of these cases we glimpse highly developed ethical practices aimed at protecting and elevating the dignity of the worker. Judaism regarded the rights of the worker as embedded in the divine plan of creation.

Similarly, Judaism did not neglect the legitimate needs of the employer. They were given the right of monetary redress against employees guilty of carelessly destroying the employer's tools, or of negligent or sloppy work (Maimonides, Sehirut 13:7). This legislation grew out of constant pre-occupation with the interactions of workers and employers. The goal was always to raise both groups to a higher sense of mutual responsibility. Better times occurred when Jewish communities, responsive to rabbinic guidance in all areas of Jewish religious life, responded also to rules governing the work place. When the Jewish ethical tradition was an integral part of Jewish life, it demonstrated a persistent ability to bring ever higher expectations into one of the basic realms of human relationships. Separated by almost two millennia from the earliest records of such efforts, we may ask if these laws were always effective. Did the realities of daily life in the work place mirror the ethical ideals?

Jewish humor provides a portrait of the gap that often marred the relationships between workers and bosses. It exploits the tensions in which the two sides are often embroiled. Jokes in this category did not have to be overly inventive. Life itself supplied the raw material. On one side were employers, forever carping about the quality of work. On the other side were the workers protesting management practices, inadequate compensation and a disagreeable work environment. These jokes speak to us from a world brimming with mutual distrust. They carry the ring of truth because they derive from real life situations. They are convincing because the clashes they describe parallel situations known to employees and employers alike. In true democratic spirit, these jokes have no favorites, assigning blame and culpability equally to either side or to both. We can read them for the easy laughs they provide; we can also see them as shrewd commentaries on human nature describing people hardly different from ourselves; people who are caught between the two poles of selfishness and a higher ethic of behavior. Reflected in them too is a brooding sadness over a world in which material progress is often accompanied by increased harshness in the work place. It is a short step to sense in these jokes a yearning for the higher standards reflected in the Jewish legal tradition.

The jokes in this section are snapshots of workers and bosses in adversarial relationships, each trying to outmaneuver and best the other, each regarding the other as no better than a necessary evil. We begin with two examples.

After closing hour, the bank's secretary and the bookkeeper left together. The secretary was barely able to contain his rage. He fumed, "I've been working for that slave driver for twenty years. I have never once opened my mouth to his constant bad-mouthing of everything I do. Today I finally lost my patience. I wrote him a really nasty letter." The bookkeeper, alarmed by what he was hearing, asked, "What did you write in the letter?" The secretary answered, "I gave it to him, chapter and verse. I left out nothing. I let him know that I've never met a bigger boor or a more arrogant stuffed shirt, and that everyone who works for him detests him!" The bookkeeper, even more alarmed, responded, "Are you out of your mind? Tomorrow, as soon as he reads your letter, he's going to fire you." The secretary grinned, "What do you mean, once he reads my letter? I said that I wrote the letter. Do you think I'm so stupid that I would actually send it to him?"

━━∽∧∼∼━━

On reaching the fiftieth year of the opening of his department store, the owner's wife, family and employees honored him at a gala banquet. Many laudatory speeches were given, and his employees presented to him a long congratulatory letter filled with many praises. After listening while the tribute was read aloud, the guest of honor responded, "My dear employees, your warm words, your praises and your good wishes have touched my heart. I want to show my appreciation and gratitude to all of

*you. I hereby present to you as my personal gift every cent you
have stolen from me all the years you have been working for me."*

—∿∿∿—

In these jokes, each side seeks a tactical advantage in a bad situation. In one story, a loyal, dedicated worker suffers from a boss
who demeans him, who omits nothing to remind him of their difference in status. What leverage does the worker have? If he threat-
ens to quit, but fails to persuade the boss to change his ways, he
could find himself in an even worse predicament. In the joke we
find him reduced to silence, frustrated to the point where he can
only talk to himself while pretending that he is speaking his mind
to his boss.

The second joke, told from the perspective of the employer, is
even more embittered. It discloses nothing of the daily encounters
between the employer and his workers. It reveals only the deep resentment that has been smoldering in the employer's heart. The sadness in the story relates to the venality of workers who cannot resist
the daily temptation to steal. In any work environment there are always devious ways to conceal the theft of money and materials.
Whether at the humblest level of work or at the highest reaches of
management, there seem always to be more and more sophisticated
means of pilfering. The temptation is ubiquitous even though short-
sighted and frequently ruinous for all who are involved.

These are two of the themes that course through the jokes in this
section. The stories come from a time and a place greatly different
from our own, but with the same behaviors that we find in our modern societies. We know only too well the misfortune of people who
cannot get along with each other, but who need each other. We
know the same dominant moods of suspicion, frustration, mistrust
and resentment that flow like a powerful tide from opposite direc-
tions, meeting to form a whirl-pool of conflict. We see in these stories an environment where cleverness is the tactic of choice and
where accommodation is equated with weakness. Missing throughout in these tales is the understanding and wisdom that coopera-
tion, mutual respect, trust and honesty will work to the benefit of all

parties. These are unhappy jokes, tinged with despair, even though they make us laugh. By depicting human relationships in a state of breakdown, these jokes are eloquent reminders of the need for commitment to ethical practices in all areas of the workplace.

MORE JOKES ABOUT WORKERS AND BOSSES

A disgruntled employee stood before his employer and complained, "I've labored for you with all my energy for the last ten years. All I ask is that you do the decent thing and give me an appropriate raise." An astonished look came over the employer's face. "Do you mean to tell me that the one hundred rubles I pay you every month isn't enough for you?" The worker replied, "For bread and butter, it suffices, but it doesn't leave me with one cent to enjoy life." His boss interrupted him, "A pay raise has nothing to do with enjoying life. If you want to enjoy life, take my advice. Try fasting for two days. You'll find out in a hurry how much joy a piece of bread will give you!"

The head of the company left his office and went out for a stroll. To his surprise, he found one of his employees walking towards him. He eyed him suspiciously and asked, "What are you doing, and where are you coming from?" The employee replied, "I'm coming back to work. I took off some time to go to the barber shop." His boss responded indignantly, "You have a lot of nerve getting your hair cut during company hours!" The employee answered, "My hair grows during working hours too."

A wealthy businessman took a dim view of one of his secretaries who regularly arrived late for work. "It's not my fault," apologized the secretary, "I'm a heavy sleeper." This angered the boss even more. "You can tell that excuse to a baby, not to me! You should follow my example. I'm up every morning at five o'clock, not at nine o'clock like you." The secretary responded, "Sir, there's no way you can compare your situation with mine. When you wake up, you know immediately that you are a rich man. You have a good reason to get out of bed early. With me it's different. Every day, when I wake up, I remind myself that I'm just a lowly, underpaid secretary. There's no reason for me to hurry to get out of bed."

⚬⚬⚬

A home owner was discussing some needed work with a repair man. He said, "I have a small hole in one wall. How much will you charge me to fix it?" The repair man examined the hole and said, "It will cost you one dollar." To which the home owner replied, "But you charged my neighbor seventy five cents to repair a much larger hole." The repair man answered, "In that case, I'll charge you seventy five cents too." The home owner was still not satisfied. He said, "Why did you first ask for a dollar?" The repair man replied, "You can't compare fixing a hole for one dollar to fixing a hole for seventy five cents. When I do a job for seventy five cents, I fix only the hole that needs to be plugged. When I charge a dollar, my fee includes holes that don't need repair."

⚬⚬⚬

A merchant suspected for some while that his cashier was stealing from the cash register. He summoned him to his office and summarily fired him. The cashier pleaded with him, "Please don't do this to me. I've worked for you for so many years. What will people say? What am I going to do? What will I say to my family?" The merchant responded, "You give me no choice. Think of what you have cost me over the years. May God add to my life a year for each and every time you have stolen from me!" The cashier retorted in anger, "I hope your prayer will be answered. May God answer my prayer too, that every extra year you receive will be filled with misery!"

BUYERS AND SELLERS

Have you ever attempted to quantify the number of daily transactions that involve commercial activities? If you are like me, it's safe to say that hardly a day passes when you are not buying something, or at least thinking about something you would like to have. The relationship between buyer and seller is not only one of our most frequent involvements, it is also one of life's most intimate experiences. The seller's goal is the sale. The buyer desires the product, but has an additional need, to be able to trust both the seller and the product. When the item we purchase falls short of its promised quality, we rightfully feel cheated, even abused. In this regard, commercial transactions, whether complex or simple, epitomize all of our interactions with other people, regardless of the context. They succeed when honesty and trust are present from start to finish, and fail when these are absent.

Our Jewish sages went to extraordinary lengths to make this point, extracting new meanings from familiar biblical texts. A biblical verse admonishes us, "Diligently heed the word of the Lord your God; do what is upright in His sight and keep His laws (Exodus 15:26)." The verse seems altogether straight-forward and direct, without any concealed meaning. Yet a second century teacher elicited a novel understanding of this command by juxtaposing "upright" with "keeping His laws." He taught that "if one is upright, that is, honest in business dealings, his fellow creatures will take delight in him, and it will be accounted to him as if he has kept all the Torah's commandments" (Mehilta, Vayassa, Chapter One). This seems an astonishing exaggeration. If we consider that the Torah comprises six hundred thirteen commandments covering a vast array of circumstances, and that many of them were further expanded into additional large numbers of rules, it seems a bizarre, even breath-taking, claim to assert that a single commandment, properly carried out in all its details, is to be considered the equal of all the other six hundred twelve combined. How are we to understand such an extreme teaching? I imagine it was meant to be an attention grabber that would cause people to seriously consider the role of ethics in the market place. Likely too, this claim was a reaction to a time when unethical business practices were rampant. Do our contemporary societies fare much better, or do we cling to the

world-weary attitude that the more things change, the more they
stay the same, and that certain ethical problems are simply endemic?
The sages of the Talmud thought otherwise. They constituted a collective gate-keeper of community behavior. They had neither patience nor tolerance for breaches of ethical conduct. They
consistently came down hard on the Jew who bifurcated his Judaism, proudly punctilious in carrying out all the details of ritual
commandments while blithely ignoring laws governing commercial relationships, whether between Jew and Jew or between Jew
and Gentile. To their mind, such a person, was a hypocrite and a
moral reprobate. The above midrashic text was a way of declaring
that the entire system of Torah, the ways we relate to one another
and the ways we relate to God, stands on a foundation of honesty.
A transaction may be as humble as purchasing a loaf of bread or as
complex as managing a far-flung global corporation, but if honesty
and trust are mocked, the entire structure of society is in danger of
collapse.

The treasury of Jewish humor contains many jokes that probe
the different ways in which buyer and seller frequently face each
other as armed combatants, each anticipating chicanery from the
other, each determined to use every wile to emerge the victor. As
only humor can, these vignettes reveal scenarios of intrigue, du-
plicity, varieties of misrepresentation and outright lies, opening to
us a door into a world we would prefer not to know. Jokes concoct-
ing farcical encounters between buyer and seller allow us to do what
polite behavior frowns upon. They make it acceptable, through the
medium of humor, to react with contempt and moral outrage to the
misdeeds of others. Jokes of this kind possess another quality, albeit
a dubious distinction. They encourage us to laugh scornfully at
someone else's moral transgressions while imagining that we are
morally superior. Our task as we hear these jokes is to listen with an
inner ear. They remind us that Jewish ethical teachings forbid us to
separate conduct we owe one another from conduct we owe to our
Creator. In their togetherness the wholeness of Judaism is achieved.
To deny one is to cripple the other.

Even as internet shopping increasingly replaces the old style of
face-to-face contact between buyer and seller, the old worries have

not gone away. Buyers remain concerned lest they be diverted by a seductive sales pitch to something different from what they wanted. They worry that once the package has arrived, the contents may be less than what was promised. The seller is equally worried about the buyer's credit worthiness. We will consider two jokes that highlight the perils of the buyer-seller relationship.

> *A wine merchant was close to death. His sons and daughters were gathered at his bedside. With his last breaths he whispered to them, "My dear children, be careful not to allow any distractions to get in the way of the wine business. No other endeavor will bring you as much profit, especially when you are making wine for the Passover holiday. I will reveal to you now the secret that has made a rich man of me and will make you rich too. You can make wine out of anything, even from grapes."*

—∽∾∿—

> *The owner of a department store had a guiding rule that he impressed upon all his employees, "Never allow a customer to leave empty-handed!" He admonished his staff that if a customer asks for an item that is in stock, it is to be given to him without delay. If, however, the customer asks for something the store does not carry, he is to be steered to something else. Every persuasion is to be used to convince the customer to buy it.*

> *A customer entered the store and asked for toilet paper. The salesman was new and unfamiliar with the store's merchandise. Not knowing where to find the toilet paper, but remembering the owner's stern warning, he said, "We seem to be out of toilet tissues, but I can give you an excellent buy on sand paper."*

These jokes display two typical risks that can subvert the buyer-seller relationship. A dishonest manufacturer or a smooth-talking salesperson can devise many "creative" ways to victimize the buyer.

Misleading advertising can present the appearance of higher quality. Inventive packaging can conceal inherent shoddiness. The wine-maker story is an example of deliberate deception. A similar deception actually occurred during the Second World War when canned salmon had all but disappeared from the civilian market in the United States, having been co-opted for the military services. There was however an inferior grade of white salmon that had been used as animal feed and fertilizer. A shrewd canner enjoyed a boom market by attaching labels that described the product as pure grade white salmon, with no artificial red coloring added. Was it a true statement? Yes. Was it outright trickery? Absolutely!

Beyond the obvious deviousness in the wine-maker story, it has a peculiarly Jewish ring. Its roots are in a time when the Passover festival created a peak season for the sale of wine. No other time of the year compared to it. Jews, as a rule, were moderate drinkers and generally limited drinking to religious ceremonies such as the Kiddush prayer welcoming the weekly Sabbath. Most Jews were unacquainted with the nuances of taste and quality in wine. Passover presented a different demand. The two Seder nights called for each participant to partake of wine four times, marking four highlight moments in the Passover ceremony. For a wine-maker, the sale of Passover wines represented a major portion of his yearly income. With this in mind, we see that several ethical breaches are involved in our story. First, there is the shamelessness of making less than pure grape wine but marketing it as the genuine product. Jewish tradition labels this kind of behavior, *g'neyvat da'at* (literally stealing another person's mind) to condemn such behavior. Second, is the total disregard of the wine's intended use as part of a religious ceremony, an especially odious indifference. Third, and worst of all, the wine-maker gleefully shares his shameful secret with his children. He savors his lifetime of cheating. His jarring death-bed command is that they follow in his footsteps as a sure path to riches. Pride in his unscrupulous ways is his true legacy to his children. The tale of the wine-maker intends to shock us as we contemplate a father whose dying wish for his children is that they become swindlers like himself.

By contrast, the second joke seems almost harmless. There is no attempt to entrap a customer into purchasing inferior goods, or to trick the buyer into gross overpayment. Here the element of trickery is the way the salesperson tries to steer the customer to something he does not need. Today we would hardly find fault with the wiles of a seller who considers toilet tissues a natural segue to sand paper. To our modern mind, a salesperson who successfully maneuvers a buyer into purchasing an unneeded item is not blamed. On the contrary, a blessing on his head and an even bigger year end bonus. We still live by the old formula of caveat emptor, let the buyer beware.

Jewish ethics separates itself from this attitude and takes a universally unpopular stance. It warns sellers against leading buyers into unnecessary purchases. But it doesn't limit itself to warning the seller alone. Buyers are warned against misleading sellers into believing that they truly wish to buy when in fact they do not. Buyers are warned against insincere bargaining or presenting themselves as solvent when they are not. The Jewish ethical understanding of buyer-seller relationships goes against the modern grain.

MORE JOKES ABOUT BUYERS AND SELLERS

A horse dealer deceived an unsuspecting buyer by selling him a lame animal. A short while later, the buyer returned and berated the seller, "Thief, cheat, deceiver! You swindled me out of my money and gave me a horse with only three good legs. Take back your miserable animal and give me back my money!" The dealer, hardly a novice in such dealings, responded, "I owe you nothing. I charged you for a horse with only three good legs."

⸺∿∿⸺

The month of Nisan arrived. Everywhere Jews were up to their necks in preparations for the coming Passover holiday. The wine-maker advertised three different varieties that would be available for the festival. A suspicious customer said to him, "It amazes me that you can sell three different wines from the same barrel." Unperturbed, the wine-maker answered, "That's nothing. From that same barrel, I can also sell vinegar."

—∿∿∿—

Mendel was frustrated. The gentile New Year had already passed and he was still left with two unsold calendars. While mulling over what to do with his inventory, he spotted Stepanski, the town mayor, walking toward him. Stepanski was a decent sort and had been one of Mendel's steady customers for years. Mendel doffed his cap to the mayor and bowed. "Your Excellency," he said hopefully, "a calendar for you, brand new, improved with all kinds of extras." The mayor declined, "Mendel, you're too late. I already have half a dozen new calendars." "Well," said Mendel, "if you have that many, one more won't hurt, and it's only a half ruble." The mayor smiled good-naturedly, "Mendel, you never give up. Go to my house and tell my wife that she should buy a calendar from you. And just to make sure that she believes that I sent you, tell her that I left my purse on the table next to the window." Before Mendel could express his gratitude to the mayor, Stepanski said, "Never mind, I just found a half ruble in my pocket." Mendel took the coin, gave the mayor a calendar, thanked him and continued on his walk....all the way to the mayor's house where he told the mayor's wife, "I've brought you a new calendar with all kinds of extras in it; it's only a half ruble." "Mendel," she exclaimed, "we don't need another calendar. See for yourself, there's one on every wall." Mendel replied, "His Excellency the mayor told me to come. He said to tell you that his purse is sitting on the table next to the window." Mrs. Stepanski sighed, took a half ruble from the purse, gave it to Mendel and took the calendar.

—∿∿∿—

Hershel the peddler often plied his trade in restaurants, hawking his wares from table to table, calling out, "Beautiful hand-

kerchiefs, gorgeous scarves, finest purses, best quality, lowest prices." The secret of his success was that he never changed his selling strategy. He relied on his skill as a pest. People would buy simply to get rid of him and then get on with their meal. On one occasion, a gentile patron of the restaurant became irritated by Hershel's sales technique. He boasted to his lunch companions, "Watch me get rid of this Jew." He beckoned to Hershel, "Hey, Jew, do you have a pair of suspenders to sell?" Hershel responded with alacrity, "Yes sir, the best quality, made from purest silk; only two rubles." The gentile said, "I'll give you one ruble. Take it or leave it." Hershel sighed, took the one ruble, handed over the suspenders, and walked away with a downcast face. The customer gloated and said to his companions, "I told you that I would get rid of the Jew. Did you see his face? He's cursing himself for not asking for three rubles."

The last two jokes, in which Jews are pitted against gentiles, merit a separate comment. Such jokes are by no means limited to commercial dealings. They share two elements: the non-Jew who has every advantage, and the seemingly defenseless Jew who resorts to guile and daring to gain the last laugh. Jokes of this type were a feature of European Jewish humor, and are best understood as an in-group response to the prevalent anti-Semitism. When Jews migrated in large numbers to America in the late Nineteenth and early Twentieth Centuries, they discovered that European anti-Semitism had been transplanted to America as well. It was relatively simple for Jews to adapt such jokes to their new environment.

The Hershel joke is sly and subtle, with Hershel seemingly the victor. After all, his sales technique proved successful once again. But is he in fact the winner? The gentile boasts that he has out-played the Jew by maneuvering him into selling the suspenders for a ridiculously low price. The joke is constructed in a way that leaves us with ambiguous possibilities. Is it perhaps a clever piece of statesmanship that allows each side to believe it has gotten the better deal?

What do Jewish ethical teachings have to say about a confrontation in which two sides are locked in a contest of mutual manipulation? Unconditionally, it declares that trickery in commerce is wrongful behavior no matter who initiates it or who is the winner. It condemns this behavior even when there is good reason to detest one of the parties. The Hershel joke is an artfully constructed piece of humor that has an after-life beyond its ostensible conclusion. It makes us reflect on our behaviors which may be within the law yet distance us from the ethical goals.

The Mendel tale takes us to a different situation. The entire story echoes a time when Jews, suffering from religious, political, economic and social disabilities, considered it a victory to best a non-Jew. Never mind that the Mendel story is a fiction. It was devised by Jews and intended for a single audience, other Jews. It permitted Jews to savor the taste of an imaginary victory, the improbable outcome of the underdog defeating the heavy favorite. Yet the underlying message is that even the smallest deception is heinous. A deceiver is a deceiver no matter how slight the sum involved or how mildly the quality of a product is overstated. And no distinction is made between Jew and non-Jew.

THE RICH IN THE EYES OF THE POOR

Poverty, with its associated miseries, is the fate of most of human kind. It has always been a concern of Jewish religion. The Torah legislated far-reaching rules to alleviate hunger, and the Prophets railed incessantly against the evils of the rich who appropriate for themselves what little the poor possess. Yet the Torah nowhere identifies wealth with wickedness. It raises no objection to the honest accumulation of personal abundance. In the same spirit, later Jewish teaching regarded wealth as a blessing, an especially useful tool for improving the lot of our fellow human beings. The Jewish verdict on wealth is that it is to be considered a gift from God requiring its possessor to meet a high standard of charity and good works.

In the Jewish view, there is no such thing as riches without obligation. The Torah sets before us a vision of an obligated society living by laws intended to narrow the economic gap separating Jew and Jew. The institution of the Sabbatical Year, possibly without precedent in the ancient world, created an astounding group of laws which cancelled unpaid loans every seventh year (Deuteronomy 15). More remarkable, the Torah grants to the poor the right to enter any privately owned field during the Sabbatical Year and to harvest its produce; in effect canceling private ownership of farm land for the duration of every seventh year (Exodus 23).

More radical still is the law that created the Jubilee Year every fiftieth year, marking the conclusion of seven Sabbatical cycles (Leviticus 25). In the fiftieth year, any land that had been sold by its original owner to settle unpaid debts reverted to the debtor or to his descendents. Historians have found no parallel to this law in other ancient legal codes.

These laws are the practical application of Judaism's theology which uniquely regards God as the ultimate owner of the cosmos. From this perspective, we are no more than temporary users, and are never to think of ourselves as the absolute owners of the earth's resources.

Taken collectively, these laws became the cornerstone of a utopian social edifice conceived to prevent the pyramiding and concentration of wealth in the hands of fewer and fewer people. They were not intended to eliminate wealth. Their goal was to plant in the soul of the Jewish people the vision of a just society, one that never stops searching for ways to adjust the economic playing field for the sake of the greatest number of its citizens. These laws were not wishful thinking or some unrealizable messianic illusion. The pages of Jewish history tell us of times when Jewish societies adhered faithfully to these obligations.

Recent history tells an opposite story. Economic revolutions have fundamentally altered the ways in which most societies function. Newer ways of amassing capital surplus have created new classes of rich and poor. Until the nineteenth century, Europe's Jews were overwhelmingly poor. Poverty, as much as anti-Semitism, led to the emigration of millions of Jews to America in the late nineteenth and early twentieth centuries. The same factors played an important role in the rise of Zionism which brought Jewish pioneers from Europe to the Land of Israel. Until these avenues of escape opened, Europe's impoverished Jews could only dream of a life in which they might know the joys of prosperity. They envied the rich. They concocted fantasies of liberation from their daily misery, but knew in their heart of hearts that poverty was destined to be their way of life. Praise was reserved only for the few among the rich who were exemplary in their giving to charity.

Enter Jewish humor. With its unique ways of looking at reality and at dreams, it cast a sharp light on the survival strategies of the poor. It found a rich potential for laughter by mocking the ways poor Jews compared themselves to the rich. Jewish humor capitalized on the schemes of penniless Jews as they imagined life with money, all the while knowing that their dreams were nothing more than games of make-believe. Many jokes in this genre taunt the simple piety of Jews who believe that with God nothing is impossible, and that if God wills it, everything can change in an instant. In these jokes, pathos rules supreme and, as often as not, the answer to the prayers of the poor is "no" or "not yet." Yiddish speaking Jews spoke of a *"bittereh gelehter"* – bitter laughter. The laughter in this chapter belongs to that category.

We examine now two jokes that reveal the struggles of Jews who search for release from the bonds of poverty.

"Please," the poor man begged his wife, "make me an omelet. The rich always eat omelets. Just for once I would like to know how an omelet tastes." His wife looked at her pleading husband and said, "How can I make you an omelet? We need eggs for an omelet, and we don't have eggs." Her husband looked at her and responded, "So let it be without eggs." She looked at him sadly and said, "How can I make you an omelet? In addition to eggs, it needs butter." His response was the same, "It will be good without butter." And so it continued; no oil, no cheese, not even a frying pan. Undeterred, the covetous husband insisted that for once in his life he must taste an omelet. With a great sigh, his wife took some flour, added water, stirred it into a paste, and poured it onto the top of the red-hot stove. When it had turned brown, she removed it, put it into a dish and set it before her husband. With rapturous joy he took a bite, swallowed it, and just as quickly spat it out. "Feh," he exclaimed, "I don't understand what the rich see in it."

—–∽∼∿∾–—

A poor Jew turned to his Rabbi for advice, "Rabbi, what shall we do? Our house is a tiny hovel; it barely stands. We have many children. We fall on top of one another, there's so little room for all of us." The Rabbi pondered the plight of the poor man and said, "Bring your goat into the house." The poor man, astonished, nevertheless did as the Rabbi advised. The next day he returned, even more distressed. "Rabbi," he cried out. It's worse than before." The Rabbi solemnly intoned, "Bring all your chickens into the house." Again the poor man did as he was told, and on the following day returned to the Rabbi, more desperate than ever. "Rabbi," he cried, "Now there's no place for us to sit." The Rabbi smiled and said, "Good; now go home and chase out the goat and the chickens." The poor man, still more confused, ran home and did as the Rabbi commanded. The next day he returned to the Rabbi and thanked him profusely, "Rabbi, we have so much room now."

~~~≈≈~~~

In both stories, the same tension is at work. The poor are trapped; they see no exit from their bleak existence. Their coping strategies are nothing more than games of make-believe, almost hallucinatory in character. Longing to savor for a brief moment the joys of the rich, the pathetic husband has melted down all of his longings to the size and taste of an omelet. His wife, the realist, knows that he is doomed to disappointment. The sadness and the despair of this story are that the poor man will end up more disconsolate than before. The punch line widens the gap between rich and poor.

In the second story, a family living in a tiny, cramped shack is trapped in its own fantasy. Salvation can only come from the Lord. They place their trust in the Rabbi; for who better than God's own messenger can perform the miracle that will save them? The rabbi's solution confirms for them that they have but one alternative, to deny their poverty by pretending that it is not real. In both tales, the people are living what Thoreau called "lives of quiet desperation."

We can be easily fooled by the deceptive simplicity of these two jokes. There is an absence of abrasive speech; there is no raging anger at life's unfairness, no murmuring of rebellion against the rich. Both stories speak in subdued tones, as if informing us that these are people who know from a lifetime of harsh experience that anger and outcry will gain them nothing.

But there is more to these stories than the sad happenstances in the lives of luckless Jews. Jews who heard these stories and laughed at them knew the Torah's demand that we must reduce the separation between rich and poor. They knew that the interpreters of the Torah dreamed of lasting solutions, dreams that are not invalidated by the length of the road that we must travel before the imbalances will be righted. These dreams are a legacy placing upon every generation of Jews the burden of making the road shorter. Jewishly, these jokes indict "business as usual" and plead for justice and fairness.

MORE JOKES ABOUT HOW THE POOR SEE THE RICH

A poor Jew was praying with great agitation. his lips moving silently, his eyes lifted high, his arms raised, and his hands gesticulating from side to side. A fellow worshipper took note of his odd behavior and said, "You look like you are having a quarrel with God." The poor man answered, "Heaven forbid. I have no arguments or complaints against the Holy One. I was merely asking a favor of God. I said to Him, Master of the universe, in the holy books it is written that in heaven a single one of Your days equals a thousand of our years. Surely then, just one of Your dollars must be the equal of a thousand of ours. So I ask You, dear Lord, what would it matter to You if You were to give me just one of Your dollars in exchange for one of mine?" The other man asked, "And how did God answer?" The poor man replied, "God told me to wait an hour."

Moshe paid a visit to a prosperous Jew hoping for a handout. The rich man obliged and asked Moshe a question, "Moshe, everyone says you're a smart fellow. So maybe you can help me understand something that's a mystery to me. I see people like you who live on handouts from people like me. But in spite of what we give them, they don't like us. Why is that so?" Moshe carefully considered the question and with great caution answered, "It's exactly the same as it is with the Angel of Death. There are people who make a living from him, but no one likes him."

A man and his wife lived in poverty; their sole possession was a scraggly old goat. He said to his wife, "We've always been too poor to give charity. I would like us to make a pledge to the charity fund that if you should die before me, I will donate the

goat's hide to the poor in your memory." Unnerved by his
words, his wife burst into tears and answered in anger, "May
God strike your tongue and make you mute!" Her husband
tried to mollify her, "Foolish one, why do you curse me? Don't
you realize that as soon as we make our pledge, we will become
just like all the rich people. They make pledges and take forever to pay them."

⁓⌇⁓

Motke, the poorest of the poor, was famed for his wit. He used
to say, "Do you know why the Rabbis compare a poor Jew to a
corpse? It's because neither the dead nor the poor should be left
unattended in a house."

⁓⌇⁓

A poor man complained, "People always say that whatever
God does is for the good. I say it's the opposite that's true.
Everything is for the worst. If my shoes have holes, water leaks
in. If my pitcher has a hole, the water leaks out."

⁓⌇⁓

A poor Jew had completed the required time of mourning for
his deceased wife. To mark the occasion, he wished to lead the
prayer service at the synagogue. As he walked to the lectern, a
rich man elbowed past him and said, "I have priority over you;
I am still within the first thirty days of mourning. At this, a
third person, also wealthy, stepped forward and announced,
"My priority is higher than both of yours; today I am observing the anniversary of the death of my father." A fourth man,
even more wealthy, pushed his way to the lectern and proclaimed, "None of you has priority over me; I am still in the
midst of the first seven days of mourning." He was about to
begin to lead the service when a pale person, robed in white, en-

tered the prayer chapel and called out in a hollow voice, "I shall lead the service; I am the deceased."

⸻

A poor man was heard to say, "Let God give me a gift of ten thousand rubles. I will immediately donate one thousand as a tithe to the poor. And just in case God doesn't trust me, let God Himself, in all His divine glory, set aside one thousand rubles for the poor, and let Him just give me the other nine thousand."

⸻

In keeping with time honored custom, a number of families obligated themselves to provide daily meals for a destitute yeshiva student. Each day of the week he was assigned to a different home for his food. Once, while sharing dinner with a host family, he was asked, "What do you pray for more than anything else?" Without hesitation he replied, "More than anything else, I pray that God should give me a gift of seven luxurious houses which I will lease to seven rich families, each of whom must agree to provide me one day's meals every week for as long as I live. That way, I will live to see heaven in my lifetime."

JEWS IN NEED
AND THEIR BENEFACTORS

The Bible's model of charity emerged in a peasant society linked to the yield of fields and orchards. The Israelite farmer was commanded to set aside a portion of the harvest for the widow, the orphan, the poor and the stranger. The practice of charity was literally a hand-to-mouth obligation for many centuries. The dispersion of Jews to Diaspora lands transformed them increasingly into urban dwellers with far-reaching consequences. One of the most profound upheavals thrust Jews into the world of money as merchants and as money lenders, the door having already been opened by rabbinic legislation that amended biblical law and permitted interest for strictly commercial loans. Both the Catholic Church and Islam held firmly to the original Jewish biblical doctrine that forbade the charging of interest in all circumstances. Neither Catholics nor Muslims were permitted to engage in money lending. By default, money lending became a Jewish profession. It is a curiosity of history that the rise of commercial banking as a driving force of economic development was a direct outcome of the role of Jews as moneylenders.

Moneylenders enjoyed a mixed reputation among fellow Jews. At best they were seen as a necessary evil. At worst they included in their ranks people who turned their backs on the poor. In addition, moneylenders were an anomaly. At a time when most Jews were poor or scarcely above the poverty line, moneylenders were conspicuously wealthy. By earning their wealth with minimal physical exertion, they appeared to be violating an older Jewish attitude that esteemed hard labor and regarded it as a virtue. Moreover, the money lender's social orbit differed radically from that of the Jewish masses. Although many Jews had some contact with gentiles, intimate access to the world of gentile culture was the exception. Moneylenders cultivated close ties with gentile aristocracy, with leaders of government and with princes of the Church. The rise of a Jewish merchant class went hand in hand with the growth of cities which attracted more and more Jews and altered the dynamics of Jewish community life. Paradoxically, Jewish poverty became even more widespread in the new urban centers than it had been in the small towns and villages of earlier times. In many jokes about Jews in need we can sense the deep yearning for a return to the Eden-like simplicity of an earlier time when a caring heart and an outstretched hand could more easily be found. Two jokes set the stage.

> *At midnight, the moneylender was startled out of his sleep by the insistent ringing of his doorbell. Alarmed, he got out of bed and made his way to the front door. Through the window, he saw a man who had borrowed money from him that same day. To the moneylender's astonishment, the man was shouting, "Tell me what time it is." The infuriated moneylender shouted back, "How dare you wake me at this ungodly hour to ask me what time it is!" The borrower replied, "What else could I do? You have my clock as security."*

> *Two Jews were involved in a dispute over a loan. They agreed to come to the Rabbi to adjudicate the case. One claimed that the other had borrowed twenty five rubles from him and now refused to pay back the loan. The other denied ever having taken a loan from him. The Rabbi resorted to a biblical precedent. He ruled that the alleged borrower must take an oath in the presence of a Rabbinic court and swear that he had not borrowed the money from the claimant. The court was convened, the oath was sworn, and the claim was denied. The lender chastised his adversary, "You are worse than a liar and a disgrace to your religion. For such a small sum, you were ready to swear a false oath!" The retort was quick in coming, "You think you are such a pious Jew. For a mere twenty five rubles you were ready to be the cause of my swearing falsely!*

These two jokes confront us with an unsavory aspect of monetary exchanges – I call it the dark side of money – that we often meet in the world of mercantile dealings, a world far removed from the biblical model of lending and borrowing. Indifference, callousness and manipulation are the common threads of these stories. In one story, the clock taken as collateral, is merely symbolic. It could as easily have been some other possession that the borrower might have needed in order to function in a normal way. The story is a stark reminder of the unevenness of the relationship in which lender and borrower meet, where the lender has the upper hand and where he can manipulate the terms of the loan as he wishes.

In the second story the borrower turns the tables on the lender, but only through an unscrupulous ploy. In this story we deal with a ruthlessly clever manipulator, a master of the system who knows how to co-opt it to his advantage. He knows that it's the nature of all legal systems to have loop holes, and he knows how to exploit the system so that an outright lie can be made to pass for the truth. The Torah's legal codes envisioned a society built upon a bed-rock foundation of truth where everyone could trust that a solemn oath sworn in a court of law would never be less than the whole truth. Here the borrower has shamelessly bilked his benefactor by converting the loan into a theft, and is not troubled in the least. The two stories, artfully disguised as humor, present to us aspects of the uses of money where strained relations are the norm, where the entire atmosphere is charged with high tension, and where the loser is not just the single victim of each tale, but society as a whole.

MORE STORIES ABOUT JEWS IN NEED AND THEIR HELPERS

Kalman says to Zalman, "Lend me ten rubles." "And why do you need ten rubles," asks Zalman. "I need it," Kalman explains," to buy some merchandise in the market. I'll sell it for fifteen, leaving me a profit of five." "In that case," says Zalman, "it would be better for both of us for me to give you five rubles. You'll have your profit immediately, and I'll come out five rubles ahead."

⌘

An immigrant Jew prospered from his hot dog stand in front of a well-known bank. One day a friend from the old country approached him and asked, "How are things with you?" The hot dog merchant replied, "God be praised. I already have enough in the bank to buy a second stand." Said the other, "In that case, do me a favor and lend me ten dollars." The hot dog merchant responded, "I'm sorry, good friend, that is something I'm not allowed to do. The bank and I have a mutual understanding. They don't sell hot dogs and I don't extend loans."

⌇⌇⌇

Two shopkeepers traveled to the big city to buy merchandise. To save on money, they agreed to share a room. All day long they were busy in the market. Late that night they returned to their room. One went to bed immediately while the other sat at the table and calculated his finances. He discovered that on the following day he would be short a hundred rubles. He called out to his companion, "Are you awake?" "Yes," was the answer. "Could you lend me a hundred rubles until we return home?" "I'm sleeping," he replied.

⌇⌇⌇

A story circulated among the merchants that a member of their group had gone insane. One of the merchants had recently lent the man a substantial sum of money. He asked in trepidation, "Does he still pay his debts?" "He's not that crazy," came the reply.

⌇⌇⌇

A textile merchant went to the big city where he purchased a large supply of cloth from a gentile dealer. The two agreed to payment of one half in cash with a promissory note of six months for the balance. The dealer was berated by the other local textile wholesalers. "You're a fool Ivan," they scolded him. "The Jew has no intention of paying you the balance. He's one of those believers who pray three times every day for their Messiah to arrive. You can bet on it that as soon as that happens, the Jew will depart for the Land of Israel and you'll lose every-

*thing he owes you." The dealer was distraught. He sought out
his customer and said to him, "I dealt with you honorably, but
you have dealt with me like a deceiver!" The Jew listened to
what the dealer had been told and said, "What they told you is
the truth. I do pray every day for our Messiah to arrive and
take us immediately back to our promised land. Even so, I assure you that you don't have to worry about the sum I owe
you. Give back to me the note I gave you, and I will give you
my written promise to pay you the entire balance the moment
the Messiah arrives.*

⌐∼∼⌐∼∼

*A Jew asks his friend, "When will you pay me back the money
I lent you?" The friend replies, "What do you think I am, a
prophet?"*

⌐∼∼⌐∼∼

*A highly esteemed member of the community determined after
reviewing his finances that he would have to renege on all the
loans he owed. Even worse, as a result of his shady financial
practices, he would not be able to return any of the moneys
that many townspeople had entrusted to him to invest on their
behalf. The next morning he informed his wife that he would
have to disappear from town until the storm over his finagling
had died down. Later that day, a poor widow came to the house
and was met by the man's wife. Unaware of the brewing scandal, the widow had brought her entire life's savings of fifty
rubles, hoping that the man would invest it for her. With great
compassion for the woman, the man's wife sought to dissuade
her. "My dear woman," she said, "my husband doesn't deal in
such small sums. You should look for someone else to invest
for you." Her husband overheard her words. He rushed from
his study and took the money from the woman, promising her
a tidy return. As soon as she left, the man's wife lashed out at
her husband, "How could you do such a thing? You're steal-*

*ing that poor woman's money. You must give it back to her."
Her husband responded with even greater anger," If she's that
poor, I'll give her a contribution; a ruble, maybe even two
rubles, but not fifty!"*

—⁓⁓—

*Two men bring their dispute before the Rabbi. One, the
claimant, says, "Rabbi, I lent him money and he refuses to
pay." The other says, "Rabbi, I'm really pinched now. This
month I am unable to make a payment." The lender responds
in anger, "That's exactly what you told me last month." The
borrower responds, "Didn't I keep my word and not pay you?"*

—⁓⁓—

*During the festival of Simḥat Torah, when Jews flock to the
synagogue to celebrate, the most disreputable Jew in the community danced passionately with a Torah Scroll. A congregant
scolded him, "How dare a sinner like you have the temerity to
dance with our holy Torah?" He replied, "You have no idea
how much I revere the Torah. If not for the Torah I would never
have made my first fortune. Some years ago I borrowed a great
sum of money and was forced to default. The lender sued me in
a Rabbinical court. The Rabbi demanded that I take an oath, as
required by the Torah. I did so and swore that I had never borrowed the money. The Rabbis had no choice but to declare me
innocent."*

As the gap between the wealthy and the poor widened, another
change occurred: a new social class arose among Jews. I character-
ize it as a new economic class. Its members were best known by the
Yiddish term *shnorrers* and even included women and children. The
shnorrers looked upon their poverty as a social credential, an iden-
tifying badge of belonging. Many among them made no pretense of
seeking gainful work. In fact, from their perspective, work would
have undermined their sense of self. In their eyes, *shnorring* was

their true calling, a profession they created for themselves through a combination of persistence and ingenuity. As urban wealth grew, and as more and more Jews became successful entrepreneurs, the numbers of *shnorrers* grew apace. In time, the members of this calling became a fixture of Jewish folk-lore. They appear in countless tales as the bane of prosperous Jews. Story after story mines a rich vein of humor by depicting wealthy Jews and *shnorrers* as combatants locked in a battle of wits whose outcome is not settled until one side has successfully outmaneuvered the other, a victory that is never more than temporary. For Jewish humorists, *shnorrer* stories offered wondrous comedic possibilities. Many of these jokes became fixtures in the lexicon of Jewish humor. We may also legitimately regard them as a barometer of a new hardness of heart reflecting the changed conditions of Jewish community life and accurately portraying the decline of older virtues.

But are *shnorrer* jokes a true mirror of the life of the Jewish beggar class? For the most part they are little more than artful deceptions which deflect us from a true appreciation of the daily misery and ego punishment of the men, women and children who were condemned to turn to others for their barest subsistence. In my view, the *shnorrer* of Jewish folk-lore hardly matches the often desperately poor person who has been beaten down by economic misfortune. *Shnorrer* anecdotes serve up a clownish figure, a master of the quick and ready retort, a consummate actor unexcelled at beguiling an evasive donor into parting with some money, however reluctantly. In *shnorrer* jokes we often meet a person who never appears defeated by the oppressiveness of his circumstances. He seems never to suffer from despair or depression. His shrewd tongue is never at a loss for a trenchant observation about the unfairness of the human condition. He seems unshakeable in his conviction that the rich need him as much as he needs them, for how else will the rich be able to fulfill the Torah's commandment to help the poor. But in truth, the *shnorrer's* tongue-in-cheek jollity barely conceals the bleak day to day existence of the beggar class.

Juxtaposed to the *shnorrer* are his counter protagonists, the rich Jew and the Jewish miser, without whom no *shnorrer* joke is worthy of its name. In shnorrer stories the rich run the gamut from the most generous to the most niggardly. Among them are paragons of hospitality and empathy. By contrast, the Jewish misers wear padlocks on their hearts, never lacking for excuses to justify why they will not help.

I believe that *shnorrer* jokes are not meant to be read as written. We should respond to them by placing a large question mark at the end of every sentence. As the joke unfolds, we should ask which would we rather be, the hungry beggar who sometimes scores a victory, or the well-off person who has the luxury of helping the *shnorrer* or turning his back on his appeal, and who in any case does not have to worry where his next meal will come from. *Shnorrer* stories are meant to make us compare our good fortune to what others do not have, and even to evoke a useful sense of guilt. *Shnorrer* jokes bring smiles to our lips; they also have the power to make us think of ourselves as potential agents of change. Our first two jokes provide a glimpse into the sad world of the *shnorrer.*

> *A rich man gives a liberal gift of money to a shnorrer. At lunch time the rich man enters his favorite restaurant. To his surprise he sees the shnorrer sitting at a table, dining on an expensive meal. The rich man bursts into anger, "You tricked me. You aren't poor after all if you can afford to eat in this restaurant." The shnorrer replies, "Why does it always have to be this way with me? When I'm broke, I can't eat in a restaurant. When I have some money, I also shouldn't eat in a restaurant. So tell me, am I never to enjoy a meal in a restaurant?"*

—◦◦◦—

> *The doctor, famed as a specialist, had finished examining a shnorrer and asked him for fifty rubles, the usual fee for his services. "I don't have that much money'" confessed the shnorrer. The disgruntled physician said, "In that case, pay me twenty five." Lamely, the shnorrer blurted out, "I have no money to pay you." The angered doctor shouted, "What nerve you have to take up my valuable time when you have no intention of paying me for my services!" "Doctor," declared the*

shnorrer, "where my health is concerned, I assure you that nothing is too good for me."

Both jokes open a window into the plight of people who carry the stigma of being beggars. It is so easy to begrudge them anything, whether a moment of pleasure or needed services, things we can have for ourselves with little effort. This is why Maimonides, the twelfth century rabbi and scholar, said in his oft-quoted step-ladder of charity that giving reaches a high level when the donor does not know the identity of the recipient and when the recipient does not know the source of the gift. It is tempting, when we place a gift into the hands of a poor person, to want to place limitations on how it may be used. It takes great wisdom to accept that the act of giving does not automatically vest in the giver the right to direct the life of the recipient. We can only hope that the gift will be wisely used, but ultimately we have to leave that decision to the person who receives it.

MORE SHNORRER JOKES

A shnorrer heard that the rich man he hoped to call on was seriously ill and about to die. He rushed to the man's home, and pushed his way to his bedside shouting, "I can save you. I have advice that can save your life." The suffering man stirred himself and pleaded, "Please help me. I will give you anything you ask." The shnorrer said to him, "Move to my neighborhood. No rich person has ever died there."

A woman and a man fell in love. He was a shnorrer and she came from a well-to-do family. She tried to persuade him to give up the life of a beggar and find another occupation. He agreed on condition that they spend their first year of marriage begging. After that, if she still insisted, he would give up the life of a shnorrer. She agreed and they spent the year wandering from town to town, begging for hand outs. At last came the day when he said to her, "Today we are married exactly one year. I am ready to give up the life of a shnorrer." She looked at the houses to the right and to the left of where they stood and said to him, "Let's finish these houses first."

⌒∿⌒

A shnorrer showed up on a Friday evening at the Synagogue. The Rabbi directed a miserly Jew to take the man home with him and to provide him with the Shabbat evening meal. The miser was a man who denied himself every luxury but one. Each week he would buy the largest, most expensive, most delicious Shabbat loaf. He ate it sparingly so that it would last him until the following Shabbat. The shnorrer had never before seen such a magnificent Shabbat loaf as the one that adorned the table. The reluctant host watched in utter dismay as the shnorrer ripped huge chunks from the loaf and devoured them. Unable to restrain himself, his host shouted, "Good man, that is not ordinary ḥallah you are eating. It's the most expensive kind that money can buy." The shnorrer responded, "Believe me, it's worth it, it's worth it."

⌒∿⌒

It was Friday evening and Shabbat was about to begin. A shnorrer accompanied by a young man entered the synagogue. The shnorrer asked the Rabbi to help him locate a home where he might have his Shabbat meals. The Rabbi agreed to help. Noticing the young man with the shnorrer, he asked who he might be. The shnorrer answered, "He's my new son-in-law. I promised to support him for a full year."

⌒∿⌒

A loud, insistent knocking was heard at the door of the rich merchant's home. A servant opened the door and saw a ragged man standing there. He refused to let him in, but the shnorrer pushed him aside, quickly entered and shouted, "Help me, I'm starving." The owner heard the commotion and decided that the best way to rid himself of the intruder was to give him a sum of money. While doling it out to him, he also lectured him, "If you weren't such an ill mannered person, I would give you twice as much." The shnorrer responded indignantly, "Sir, you are a merchant. I know nothing about being a merchant. I don't give you advice about how to run your business. I'm a shnorrer. Don't tell me how to run my business."

—⁓∿⁓—

Some shnorrers were blessed with the good fortune of patrons who helped them repeatedly. A shnorrer entered the office of a donor who gave him the same generous sum year after year. This time, he was stunned when he received a mere token amount. His benefactor explained, "I have unusual expenses this year. I am marrying off my daughter. The wedding will be very costly. I will also be paying for their honeymoon cruise, a trip around the world. I'm also purchasing for them a home and two automobiles. I cannot help you this year as I have in the past." The shnorrer responded with great indignation. "Support your family with your own money, not with mine!"

THE JEWISH CIVIL SERVICE

Contemporary American Jewish communities differ vastly from those in the recent past. Today a typical Jewish community is defined by an impressive array of institutions, religious and secular, and by communal services that were hardly known to our forebears. We depend on an army of Jewish professionals; social workers, executive directors, educational specialists, fund raisers and activity leaders for all age and interest groups to keep the gears of our institutions turning. Even the clergy, the professionals with the longest history, differ greatly from their counterparts of the past, for the simple reason that the American synagogue is a radically different institution. The neighborhood congregation of my youth was exclusively a prayer house. When the daily prayer service ended each morning the building was locked tight and did not reopen until the evening service, after which it was locked again. Not so long ago, the picture was very different. Jews lived under a narrower umbrella of concerns. The core values of Jewish life came largely from religious beliefs and practices, and Jews depended upon a small, more informal cluster of civil servants. They included the *rabbi*, the *hazan*(cantor), the *shammes* (sexton), the *melamed* (religious studies tutor), the *shohet* (ritual slaughterer), the *mohel* (circumciser), and the *sofayr* (scribe). They were the guardians and transmitters of all that Jews held sacred. I think of them as the "civil service" of the Jewish world of their time. A Jewish community bereft of any of them felt itself to be spiritually diminished.

In addition, there were those who served as fringe professionals, significant and colorful in their own way. Notable among them were the *shadhanim* (matchmakers) and the *m'shulahim* (traveling solicitors for a variety of community causes). Collectively, all of them were heroes of Jewish continuity, true servants of God and of their fellow Jews. Often self-sacrificing in the fulfillment of their duties, they were revered as exemplars of piety. Nevertheless, their ranks also included charlatans who posed behind a mask of false piety. At times, leaders are prey to the temptation to overstep their bounds. Leaders may lure themselves into believing that no one is better suited or more deserving of their high status. Vulnerable to hubris, they may come to regard themselves as above their community, possessing greater entitlements and immunities. Especially during times of social upheaval, the door was open to deceivers and incompetents .In particular, isolated Jewish communities, remote from the main Jewish centers, might fall victim to imposters who claimed the requisite qualities of knowledge and spiritual integrity.

The stories assembled here have traveled to us from older, simpler times. Even so, we find in them similarities to problems that continue to plague us. Now, as then, leaders have to be held to a high standard of behavior. What passes for an easily forgotten minor infraction when done by an ordinary citizen, is considered more serious when committed by a leader. See what happened to Moses when he had an outburst of public anger. God had instructed him to speak to a rock so that water would miraculously pour forth for the thirsty people. Instead he lost his temper and harshly belittled them for their impatience and lack of faith. An ordinary person would have earned a mild rebuke at most. Yet for this momentary loss of self-control, Moses was severely punished. He was denied the fulfillment of his most precious dream, to lead his people into the Promised Land. .

Every culture has well-rehearsed jokes that belittle their leaders, and Jewish humor is no exception. It may not be richer than other traditions in this regard. However, Jewish humor takes special delight in ridiculing the grossly unqualified community servant. There is a tone of outraged indignation in these jokes, as if they are demanding, "Who are you to present yourself as qualified for such a calling?"

Among those who make up our Jewish civil service, we single out the *rabbi*, the *ḥazan*, the *shammes* and the *melamed*.

> *A rabbi of limited abilities, but possessed of unlimited ego, hoped to advance his career by writing a book. He assembled a collection of his sermons and brought it to a famous scholar to seek his endorsement. The scholar agreed to examine it. After perusing several pages, he came to the conclusion that it was a work of no merit. Not wishing to hurt the writer's feelings, he took a sheet of paper and wrote at the top, "I heartily recommend this worthwhile book." At the bottom of the paper, he signed his name, leaving a large empty space in between. The*

Rabbi read his comments and was both elated and confused. He asked, "Why did you leave so much empty space between your words of praise and your signature?" The scholar replied, "I did so to fulfill the Torah's commandment, 'You shall keep far from an untruth' (Exodus 23:7)"

≈≈∿∾≈

A certain ḥazan greatly admired his own singing voice. It was but one example of his lack of all humility. At the end of the Rosh Hashanah service, he sought a compliment from the president of the congregation, "What did you think of my singing today?" The president, well aware of the ḥazan's limitless vanity, replied, "I was dazzled by your amazing memory." Puzzled by the president's words, he asked, "What has my memory got to do with my singing?" The president answered, "You made the identical mistakes this year that you made last year."

≈≈∿∾≈

A Jew entered a restaurant to have his lunch. It happened to be a day of obligatory fasting for Jews. To his surprise and indignation, he saw a familiar person having a sumptuous meal, none other than the shammes whom he had engaged and paid to fast on his behalf, (this custom was once practiced by Jews who found themselves unable to fast). *In a great huff he marched over to the shammes and berated him, "Scoundrel, deceiver! Is this how you fast on my behalf?" The shammes, not at all perturbed, rose to his feet and explained, "It's not what you think, no matter how it looks. It so happens that Cohen the butcher also hired me to fast for him today, but he has refused to pay me the agreed upon sum. I am eating to protest his unethical behavior. I want him to know that he cannot treat me that way. But rest assured that I am fasting for you."*

≈≈∿∾≈

The Talmud is replete with closely reasoned discussions in which complex legal questions are minutely analyzed from every possible angle. In many such discussions, a favorite question asks, "And what would we decide if the situation were reversed." A certain melamed who liked to impress his students with his own cleverness often resorted to this question. On one occasion, the class was studying the ruling regarding a wedding day on which a parent of either the bride or the groom suddenly dies. The ruling is that the wedding should go on as planned. Suddenly the melamed confronted the students with a question, "And what if the situation was reversed and it was the bride or the groom that died?"

━━◦◦◦◦━━

The leader-servants in these stories have much in common. Each of them provides an essential service to the community. They possess an authority sanctioned by age-old custom. Regardless of personality and individual style, they were expected to be knowledgeable and properly trained. Their communities expected them to believe in the sacred meaning of their work. When one of these civil servants was found to be unworthy of the community's trust, the effect was demoralizing.

In this group of stories a *rabbi* whose need to be admired and celebrated cannot disguise his less than adequate knowledge. His counterpart, the *ḥazan*, so much adores the sound of his own voice that it matters little to him that he mispronounces the prayers he chants. The *shammes*, who was expected to perform personal acts of kindness, resorts to glibness to cover his deception. The *melamed* fails a key test of a genuine educator. He would rather display his cleverness than help his students deal with a painful issue. Hypocrisy, ego and laziness drive the key actors in these stories, abusing the people who have placed their trust in them.

It is but a short step to other stories about impostors with false titles who ascend to positions to which they are not entitled. I was once told of a person who served a small community as its rabbi. Mysteriously, when he left the community he left behind what peo-

ple had thought was his certificate of ordination. The Hebrew text
was translated for them one day:

> "To all concerned, regarding the person about whom
> you have inquired, whose English name is _____, and
> who is known also by the Hebrew names _____, and
> who claims to have been a student in our institution and
> to have completed all requirements for ordination be it
> known to all that we have diligently searched our
> records and must regretfully inform you that said per-
> son was at no time a student in our Rabbinical Seminary,
> let alone the recipient of ordination from us. Signed by
> Rabbi _____, Dean."

This story has many close relatives, all attesting to the devious
means practiced by fakers, charlatans, and swindlers, who successfully beguiled many unsuspecting souls into accepting them as genuine. They were never more than a small percentage of the Jewish
"civil service," but unfortunately they left a stain in their wake.

Cleverly crafted Jewish humor provokes us into laughing at the
unqualified people who pretend to be what they are not. It assumes
that they deserve to be held up to public scorn. Where jokes about
our Jewish civil service are concerned, Jewish humor wholeheart-
edly invokes the wisdom of contemporary news media: an obedient
dog is not newsworthy, but a dog that bites its master is. We find
few Jewish jokes about the loyal, ably qualified civil servants who
faithfully and honorably discharge their tasks. They concentrate instead on the impostors. By exposing the unqualified, unworthy, ego-
driven civil servant, they honor the idealistic one.

MORE STORIES ABOUT THE JEWISH CIVIL SERVICE

*In the synagogue, on the concluding day of the Sukkot festival,
the ḥazan was about to begin singing the special prayer for
abundant rain. Suddenly the skies blackened and unleashed a
savage downpour, continuing without let-up until the service
concluded. The ḥazan boasted to the congregation's president,"*

Today the heavens heard my beautiful singing and immediately answered with rain!" The president, well aware of the ḥazan's insatiable ego, responded, "It was no surprise. The Torah tells us that once before, people like you caused a great flood to come."

—∿∿—

Every year, the shammes called on a certain wealthy Jew to remind him that the yahrzeit, the anniversary date of the death of his father, was coming. Without fail, the wealthy man rewarded the shammes generously. The shammes, always enterprising where his own benefit was concerned, saw an opportunity to profit even more. Knowing that his benefactor was occupied with business matters day and night, he began to call on the rich man twice annually as a reminder. Each time the response was generous. When the man's mother died, the shammes began calling upon him two additional times to remind him of her yahrzeit as well, and expected to be rewarded amply for his solicitousness. His plan backfired. The rich man saw through the scheme and told him, "A person is not always certain of who his father is, so a double reminder is acceptable. But I know who my mother was. One reminder is sufficient. For the other one you get nothing."

—∿∿—

The children were studying with their melamed the portion of the Torah which describes the aftermath of the escape of the Hebrew people from their slavery in Egypt. The Torah says that the news of their miraculous deliverance quickly spread throughout the region and that "Jethro, Priest of Midian, father-in-law of Moses, heard it." (Exodus 18:1). One of the children was puzzled by the description of Jethro's occupation. "Teacher," he asked, "How could Jethro have been Moses' father-in-law if he was a priest? Aren't priests forbidden to marry and have children?" The melamed was stumped by the child's question, but quickly regaining his composure he replied, "My child, obviously this happened before the laws of the Torah were given."

<hr>

An advanced class was studying Talmud with a melamed who was less than advanced. Their topic was the section dealing with the laws of Passover. Among the foods considered acceptable for the seder ceremony, the Talmud mentions one called "tamha," (B. Pesaḥim 39a). One of the students asked, "What is the meaning of tamḥa? The melamed, not too sure himself how to translate the word, immediately instructed him to look it up in the Rashi commentary. The child did as he was told. He saw that Rashi had written, "This will be explained later in the chapter." He turned the pages and saw that the Talmud quotes the cryptic words of a sage who explains that "tamḥa is the same as tamaḥta." Again the student questioned the Melamed, "Teacher, what is tamaḥta?" The teacher impatiently responded, "Did I not tell you to read what Rashi says?" The student replied, "I did look at the Rashi comment, and he says "tamaḥta is the same as maruvia." (Rashi, a resident of France in the 12th century, frequently uses old French to explain Talmudic terminology). *The student, now more puzzled than before, asked again, "But what is maruvia"? The melamed, exasperated by the child's questions and frustrated by his own ignorance, blurted out, "Go ask a Frenchman!"* (Note: Tamḥa is a bitter herb which can be used during the Seder ceremony.)

<hr>

A high government official paid a visit to the town. To honor him, all of the community leaders gathered at the train station to welcome his arrival, the melamed among them. The official exchanged pleasantries with the members of the welcoming committee. Turning to the melamed, he asked, "How many

children do you have?" The proud melamed answered, "With
God's help, I have thirty seven." The official roared with laugh-
ter. The melamed realizing that he had misunderstood the ques-
tion, corrected himself, "Sir, not all by myself. I have a helper."

—∿∽—

In the synagogue study room, a group of men, the melamed
among them, digressed from their text and pondered aloud how
rich the fabled millionaire Rothschild really was. Each of them
ventured a different estimate. The melamed expressed his own
opinion on the matter. He said, "I don't know how rich Roth-
schild is, but if I had as much money as he has, I would be even
richer. I would do a little teaching on the side."

—∿∽—

A father hired a melamed to teach his son for a full year. They
agreed that the melamed would be paid once a month. After
the first day, the melamed insisted that the father pay him for
the entire year in advance. The father demanded an explana-
tion. Not wishing to tell the father that his son had limited
intelligence, he replied, "It once happened to me that a child I
was tutoring died shortly after the first lesson. As a result, I
lost a great deal of income." The father was not satisfied by
the melamed's answer. He asked further," But what if I pay
you in advance for the entire year and you should suddenly
die?" The melamed replied, "In that case, I would come out
ahead."

—∿∽—

A certain Jew posed as a rabbi. He began to think of himself as
more learned than he was, and hoped to gain fame by writing
a commentary to poems of lamentation that are traditionally
recited on the ninth of Av, marking the destruction of
Jerusalem and its holy Temple at the hands of the Romans. He

sent his manuscript to a highly regarded professor known for his vast scholarship, and waited to receive his recommendation. The manuscript was returned along with the professor's evaluation, "I have read your commentary on the poems of lamentation. It too is lamentable."

~~~

A group of friends were exchanging stories. One asked, "Have you heard the news about Yankel the stammerer? He moved to America and got himself a job as a <u>h</u>azan." One of the friends responded, "It's happened before. The Torah says that Moses too was a stammerer, but as soon as he led the Jews to safety across the Reed Sea, he began to sing." (The reference is to the Song of Moses that followed the miraculous crossing of the sea: Exodus ch.15.)

~~~

Jokesters were fond of asking, "How many fools are there among Jews?" Answer, "No one knows the precise number, but we can say for sure that they are not less than ten percent because whenever a group of ten Jews gather to pray, at least one of them claims to be a <u>h</u>azan."

~~~

We conclude this section with two shaggy dog stories. The pleasure of such stories is the challenge to guess the final outcome before reaching it.

The melamed wanted his pupils to understand the complicated ways in which money directs the lives of people and separates the rich from the poor. The melamed was, of course, completely naïve about the subject. He said to them, "Think of a simple, ordinary Jew. He puts on a clean shirt only once a week, in honor of Shabbat. A rich Jew, on the other hand, puts on a fresh shirt every day. Rothschild, the great millionaire, changes his shirt three times a day. Most blessed of all is the Kaiser. Two soldiers stand at his side; one dresses him in clean shirts, and one undresses him, all day long.

An ordinary person takes a single lump of sugar to sweeten his cup of tea. A rich man uses no less than three. Rothschild puts three lumps into his cup and three into his mouth. The Kaiser's servants pour his tea into a keg of sugar, and he drinks directly from it.

An ordinary person spreads a bit of butter on a roll. A rich man spreads butter inside the roll and on the outside. Rothschild spreads butter on the inside and on the outside after each bite. Two waiters stand alongside the Kaiser. Each holds a butter knife. While one spreads chunks of butter on the inside of the roll, the other spreads chunks on the outside.

An ordinary person eats a donut just as it is. A rich one dips his donut into a hot sauce and eats it. Rothschild dips his donut into the sauce before every bite. The Kaiser wears a special jacket with many deep pockets. Some of the pockets are crammed with donuts and others are filled with hot sauce. When it pleases him, he takes a donut from one pocket, dips it into the hot sauce in another pocket, and eats.

An ordinary person's wife sees to it that no one interrupts his sleep. A rich man's home has many bedrooms, with one of them far removed from the others; he sleeps there undisturbed. Rothschild has twelve guards who stand watch at the door to his bedroom to prevent anyone from interfering with his sleep. The Kaiser has an entire legion of soldiers who surround his bedroom and shout all night long," Silence! Silence! The Kaiser sleeps!"

An ordinary person rises from his sleep early in the morning and has a bite to eat. A rich man rises at ten in the morning *and is served his breakfast. Rothschild lies in bed until the afternoon hours when he rises and eats. The Kaiser sleeps all day and all night and doesn't have his breakfast until the next day."*

⁓⌇⁓

When the Holy One, Praised be He, set about to create the universe, His first thought was to allocate the same life span, forty years, to all creatures. Soon after He completed the work of creation, a parade of creatures, led by the horse, assembled before the Holy One's majestic throne. The horse approached the Creator and asked, "O Lord, to every creature You have assigned a task. What is to be my task on earth?" The Holy One looked kindly at the horse and replied, "Humans will ride upon your back." The horse heard the Holy One's words, neighed and shook his head from side to side, and responded, "In that case, twenty years will suffice for me." The Holy One agreed and allotted to the horse and to its descendents a life span of twenty years. Next to appear before the throne of God was the mule who inquired, "What, O Holy One, shall be my task on earth?" The Lord replied, "You shall be a beast of burden, and you and all of your descendents shall live for forty years" The mule shook his head vigorously and said, "If that is to be my fate, I too wish to live for not more than twenty years." The Lord agreed to this request too. Next arrived the hazan. He approached the throne of God and asked, "What shall be my task on earth?" God answered, "Your calling will be the most pleasant of all. You will be a singer of sweet melodies, and you will lead all who listen to you to love Me with all their heart, soul and mind. Forty years will also be your span of life." The hazan was both pleased and displeased. "O Lord," he implored, "If that is to be my calling on earth, forty years will not suffice. I implore You, dear Lord, to add an additional forty years to my life." The Holy One agreed to his request. He added to the hazan's life the twenty years taken from the horse and the twenty years taken from the mule. The proof is that to this day people like to say, "For the first forty years, a ḥazan's voice is sweet and pleasant. For the next forty, he neighs like a horse and brays like a mule."

.

THE LEARNED AND THE IGNORANT

The need to elevate some people to high status must be as old as human society. We build the highest pedestal so that the winner of an Olympic event can tower above the second and third place finishers, and we do the same for the people in our communities we regard as winners.

How one acquires elevated status is part of the legacy of every social group. Political success, military heroism, charismatic leadership qualities and intellectual achievement, are typical stepping stones to fame. Stardom in the tinsel world of entertainment can open a magic door to public acclaim. Personal wealth, gained through hard work or by the less onerous route of family inheritance, may also crown its possessor with high status. In the not distant past, being born into a family possessing hereditary aristocratic rank automatically conferred high status. Regardless of the chosen path, all societies have their favored ways of transforming certain people into larger than life.

Within Jewish experience, the path to prominence has been both similar and vastly different. Ordinary Jews, like citizens of all communities, take pride in Jews who attain high levels of success as military heroes, captains of industry, entertainers and athletes, and shower them with great honor. On the other hand, the teachers of Judaism championed a radically different model of success. They looked askance at the conventional ways of granting and receiving acclaim and had a simple criterion for those worthy of honor.

The critical factor was durability. Fame resulting from transient circumstances failed to meet that test. The athlete or the entertainment idol whose youthful prowess or beauty fades with time does not make the grade. Wealth, no matter how amassed, may be lost to economic forces beyond control. Time and again we find the Jewish sages comparing the vicissitudes of life to a wheel that is forever turning, now up, now down; sometimes bestowing good fortune and sometimes stealing it away. According to the durability test, transient achievements that last for only a fraction of a lifetime do not merit honor.

For as far back as we have reliable historical records, the Sages bestowed their highest accolades upon the Jew who engaged in lifelong study of Torah, a never-ending quest for spiritual knowledge.

People who reach such heights are not diminished by the vagaries
of time, place or fortune. As receivers and transmitters of the best of
Jewish tradition, they become living bridges, connecting us to our
past and our future. The majority of Jews who did not live by these
standards nevertheless knew who the real heroes were, and conferred their greatest adulation on those who made the study of
Torah their main passion.

Paradoxically these same Jewish heroes often succumbed to arrogance at the expense of Jews who did not match their learning.
We see evidence of this attitude in the Talmud where sages are described as advocating that a learned Jew should scrupulously avoid
the company of a Jewish ignoramus while on a journey (BT Pesaḥim
49b). Even Hillel, the master sage famed for many humane teachings, taught that "an ignoramus can never achieve true piety"
(Mishna Avot, Chapter 2). There were scholars who understood the
harm in this attitude. They taught, "Never say that we should re-
strict our love to students (of Torah), and show no love to unlearned
Jews; we must love them both" (Avot D'Rabi Natan, Chapter 16).
By cultivating a sense of self-superiority, many in the Jewish learned
class inflicted emotional damage upon ignorant Jews.

The gulf separating the learned and the unlearned was an irresistible opportunity for Jewish humor. The same jokes also present
us a challenge with significant ethical implications.

Consider two representative jokes.

*An ignorant Jew became wealthy. He immediately gave a sub-
stantial gift to the synagogue and acquired for himself a pres-
tigious permanent seat at the eastern wall of the sanctuary
where the most learned members of the community sat, including the Rabbi of the congregation. On the first occasion
when he occupied his seat, he noticed that all the people who sat
at the eastern wall wrapped their taleysim (prayer shawls)
around their heads while reciting the prayer for donning the
tallis. He observed their procedure carefully and did as they
did, not realizing that this was the custom of only the most
learned and ultra-pious Jews. The Rabbi, who occupied the ad-
joining seat, took note of his behavior and said to him, "I infer*

from how you covered your head with your tallis that you too must be a very learned Jew. That astonishes me. How can it be that someone as learned as you does not know that a Jewish ignoramus does not cover his head with the tallis?"

⌇⌇⌇

A Jewish saloon keeper, proud but ignorant, was determined to raise his son with Jewish knowledge. He hired a learned tutor to teach the child the Hebrew language. The boy, as it happened, was quite slow-witted. One day the father saw the tutor laboriously repeating the words of the Kaddish (the mourner's prayer) with the child. He became indignant and accosted the tutor, "How dare you teach my son a prayer to mourn my death?!" The tutor responded, "Don't worry. You'll be a very old man by the time your son masters the words of the Kaddish."

These are two pathetic stories, dressed up as jokes. What they share is their choice of victim, in each case a person of limited knowledge, a Jewish ignoramus. The newly rich know-nothing in the first tale is mocked for his intellectual poverty and for crossing a social boundary by no less a person than the Rabbi. In the second story, the unstated obvious message is that ignorance breeds ignorance; like father, like son. In neither story are the protagonists given the slightest credit for decent intentions.

MORE JOKES ABOUT THE LEARNED AND THE IGNORANT

A worried Jew, something of an ignoramus, met a friend who immediately recognized that something was troubling him. In response to his query, he replied, "My wife has been in labor for two weeks and is in great distress." His friend said, "I know a remedy for her. We can do it for her immediately. All we need are ten pious men to gather at her bedside and recite the Book of Psalms." The grateful husband quickly rounded up a group of ten men and brought them to his wife's room where they began to recite Psalms. A few minutes later the midwife shooed them out of the room. Within moments she emerged, shouting to the husband, "Good news! Your wife has given birth to a son." The husband ran to the bedroom, but was stopped at the door by the midwife, "You cannot enter just now. She's in the middle of delivering a second one." The same thing happened a third time. Noticing that the ten men were still reciting Psalms aloud, he shouted to them, "Stop reciting immediately!"

—◇◇◇—

Through a stroke of unexpected good fortune, an ignorant laborer became wealthy. Along with his sudden elevation to a life of riches, he soon acquired among his friends a reputation for wisdom. After some years, disaster struck; he lost all of his wealth and became a poor laborer once again. He was able to deal with the change in his material fortunes, but soon discovered that his acquaintances no longer considered him wise. He complained bitterly to his wife, "That my wealth is gone I can understand, but that people should think that because I am penniless my wisdom too has left me, this I cannot understand."

—◇◇◇—

A Jewish peasant, bereft of any Jewish upbringing, traveled from his tiny village to the city to celebrate Rosh Hashanah (the Jewish New Year holiday) with other Jews. During the recitation of one of the prayers, he saw all the congregants turn towards the east and prostrate themselves. Seeing them stretched out on the floor, he did the same, but faced to the west. The Jew next to him said, "You're doing it the wrong way. Turn around." The peasant rolled onto his back.

—◇◇◇—

Isaac the wagon driver was well up in years. His days were long and hard, and he barely eked out a living hauling heavy loads from place to place. He was perpetually exhausted. Often he would pause during his labors, lift up his head to the heavens, and exclaim with a sigh, "Lord of the universe, how blessed is your gift of the Sabbath to your children, the people of Israel. In Your great mercy, You have bestowed upon us one day each week that we might rest and recover from the woes of our daily labors. Were it not for this precious gift, we could not survive. What a pity, dear God, that You ordained in Your holy Torah that the Sabbath must come at the end of the week when I am too worn out from my labors to enjoy it. What would it hurt, dear Lord, if You would arrange for the Sabbath to come in the middle of the week?"

<center>~~~~</center>

On several Jewish holidays, it is the custom to add a group of Psalms known as Hallel (praise) to daily prayers. On some holiday mornings, the entire group, the full Hallel, is recited. At other times, a shortened version, the half Hallel, is recited. Two Jews, unfamiliar with prayer traditions, and knowing only that the full Hallel is recited on some occasions and the half Hallel on other occasions, were nevertheless in agreement that Hallel is added to the prayer service on the holiday of Purim, when in fact it is not. They argued over one issue: Is it the full Hallel or the half Hallel? One asserted, "On Purim we are required to recite the full Hallel." His companion responded with equal conviction, "Not so! Purim is the same as Rosh Ḥodesh (the first day of a Jewish calendar month, regarded as a semi-holiday) when we recite only the half Hallel." A third Jew, just as unlearned, overheard the conversation and corrected the two men, "What ignoramuses you are! Listen to me. Everyone knows there are two rules regarding Hallel on Purim. The first rule is that only when Purim coincides with Rosh Ḥodesh (an impossibility because Purim falls on the 14th of Adar) that we recite the half Hallel. But when Purim occurs during the week of Hannukah (three months earlier than Purim in the month of Kislev), that is when we recite the full Hallel."

Judaism, through its ethical system, mandates extreme caution with regard to the spoken word, and this is precisely what these stories violate. The Talmud interprets the Torah's warning, "Keep far from any wicked thing" (Deuteronomy 23:9) as a prohibition against uttering insulting words (BT Ketubot 46a).

Jokes at the expense of Jews who know little of their Jewish heritage are clearly meant to shame them. They capitalize on a knee-jerk response that virtually guarantees our laughter. They illustrate our proneness to step on the dignity of another person, violating both the letter and the spirit of Jewish ethical teachings. These jokes are in essence sad commentaries on our imperfect selves. In an ideal world, no one would tell them; they might not exist at all. Until that time, we can utilize them as exhortations to restrain ourselves from making targets of those who know less than we do.

CITY SLICKS
AND SMALL TOWN HICKS

When we think about city life versus small town life, we tend to think that cities are the more dynamic places, offering greater varieties of work, education and culture. It is the city, so we imagine, that is always the incubator of social revolution, whereas in the small town people hold tenaciously to old patterns of life, locked into habit, suspicious of change.

Despite this conventional stereotype, there is good evidence from Jewish history, especially of ancient Israel, that the opposite was often the case. Agriculture, more than industry, was the primary engine of wealth. The wealthy Jews lived where they produced their wealth, in the country-side. By contrast, the poorest Jews, society's most underprivileged, were crowded into cities where few opportunities were available to them. How Jews educated their children provides a telling illustration of the differences between urban and small town Jewish life.

In the ancient period Jewish learning was almost the exclusive birth right of Jewish males but was largely restricted to the sons of the wealthy. No one was a better spokesman for this tradition than the illustrious sage Shammai who lived two thousand years ago. Shammai, one of the greatest Israeli interpreters of Jewish religious law, proclaimed that serious Jewish schooling should be offered only to the sons of the rich. We have no reason to believe that he was biased against the poor, that he considered them inherently inferior. His reasoning was altogether pragmatic. The rich could afford to educate their sons. The poor simply lacked the means. Their sons were needed at an early age to add their scant earnings to the family's meager resources.

Shammai's patrician attitude was opposed by Hillel, the great sage who contested Shammai's teachings in many areas of Jewish law. From all evidence, Hillel was a person of almost no means, more at home with the poor than with the economically comfortable. Hillel struggled against the status quo. He opposed the accepted reality of a culture which relegated the poor and their children to a voiceless role in Jewish society. Hillel insisted, "Be solicitous of the sons of the poor, for it is they who shall be the source of Torah knowledge." Hillel knew intimately the choking environment of Jerusalem's slums where teeming masses of Jews had almost no prospect of educating their children, lacking even the space to erect a sukkah. Hillel sparked a cultural upheaval, a spiritual revolution that made serious Jewish learning available to the poor. It is a proud foot-note of Jewish history that ultimately his doctrine prevailed and became a norm of Jewish community responsibility.

However, history does not always advance in a straight line. Closer to modern times, in centers of Jewish dispersion in many lands, large cities became the engines of change, the prime movers of new industry and of culture. Among Jews, small towns and villages became back-water settlements of Jewish knowledge, with Jews constituting one element of a peasant population. In Eastern Europe, in Poland especially, there were hundreds of such villages where Jews lived for generations. In many they were even the majority ethnic group.

The word for village in Yiddish is *shtetl,* but it carries a large baggage of meaning. *Shtetl* Jews were generally unsophisticated. For the most part they were religiously observant, without knowing the basis of their piety. Jewish schooling in such villages was either nonexistent or at a low level. The master Yiddish story-teller, Sholom Aleichem, created the unforgettable character, Tevyeh the milk peddler, as the embodiment of the *shtetl* Jew. Tevyeh has only scant Jewish knowledge and is unable to provide a rationale for even the simplest Jewish religious practice. When challenged, his best answer is that it is a "tradition."

Cities with large Jewish populations had the best Jewish schools and attracted the most learned teachers and rabbis. Yiddish, the natural idiom of Eastern European Jews, used the term *dorf's yid* – literally, a hamlet Jew – as the unflattering designation of the village Jew, a country bumpkin, something of a simpleton and, above all, an ignoramus. As we might expect, by contrasting city and village types, Jewish folk-lore feasted on the abundant tensions between the Jewish city slicker and the Jewish small town hick. As we have already seen, Jewish jokes often have as an external purpose poking fun at other Jews, but frequently have a second, concealed agenda. They admonish us that it is unethical to demean a fellow human being and to seek laughter at the expense of another person's dignity.

We begin with two jokes that typify the extreme oppositeness of city slicks and small-town hicks.

> *A shtetl Jew arrived in the big city on a Friday. It was his first experience away from his home town. The next morning he set out on foot to attend Shabbat prayers. On his way to the synagogue, he passed a number of Jewish merchants who sat in front of their open shops waiting for customers to arrive. For them, the Shabbat was no different than any other day of the week. Shocked and confused by what he saw, he continued on his way. A store keeper saw him and called out, "Come in. All men's suits are available at seventy percent off." Greatly upset by this desecration of the Shabbat, the visitor shouted back, "Shame on you! Isn't it enough that you are violating the Shabbat? Must you also announce it for the whole world to hear?" The store keeper shot back, "I'm forced to sell good quality suits at seventy percent off, and you call that doing business on Shabbat?!"*

This joke like the tip of an iceberg, barely hints at a much larger and deeper background. To understand that background, we have to ask what inner qualities the village Jew brings with him that sets him at odds with city Jews. Is it that he is religiously observant, whereas in the city he encounters Jews who have long since abandoned the practice of Jewish rituals? It includes that, but goes deeper still. In his *shtetl*, he does not stand out as different or deviant in any way. On the contrary, his sense of himself as a Jew and the personal strength he receives on his home ground, are rooted in the knowledge that he and his neighboring Jews share the same pattern of Jewish expression in all of its details. They practice identical rituals. On the Shabbat and Festivals, they rest from work in the same way. At home he and his companions are identical, interchangeable parts of a single spiritual organism in which each one contributes to the wholeness of the fabric of Jewishness. But once in the city, his world is turned upside down. He is unable to grasp what, if anything connects him to Jews who do not share in what he considers sacred. His confusion gives way to anger, and he lashes out with condemnation.

The city Jew, similarly, has neither a kind thought nor a friendly word for the village Jew, and dismisses him derisively as an ignoramus and a boor. This is a story that could be told in a number of different ways, employing a wide variety of conflict situations to dramatize the extreme separation between the two types of Jews. The Shabbat is frequently the foil for their mutual disdain. Each side responds with scorn and builds on the temptation always close at hand, to justify ourselves by dismissing those who differ from us. It utilizes the familiar technique of the put-down, but its real purpose is to inflate our sense of our own worth. The Sages of the Mishnah cautioned, "Don't be guilty of judging your fellows until you stand in their place." It is easy to condemn others and it is tempting to beguile ourselves into believing that our way is the only way. The serious message of this joke is that angry speech, more often than not, achieves nothing.

The next joke presents the small town Jew in another unfavorable light.

> *A Jew from a tiny town made his first visit to the city. For the first time in his life, he entered a restaurant and asked to be served a meal. The waiter gave him a menu and quickly realized that he was dealing with a naïve country yokel. He brought him a plate of reheated, stale leftovers. After finishing his meal, the customer left the restaurant and soon developed a terrible stomach-ache. He entered an alley where he brought up the entire meal. A policeman spotted him and fined him ten rubles for dirtying city property. The Jew became confused. "Officer," he said, "I don't understand this. It cost me one ruble to buy a meal. Should it cost me ten rubles to throw it up?"*

These stories, like all of the stories in this unit are distortions, deliberately one-sided and misleading portrayals of small town Jews. They ignore the truth that villagers can be as complex and many-sided as urban dwellers. A hamlet as well as a metropolis can produce saints. Evil in its many manifestations can strike roots in both a shtetl and a city. These are stories with a common feature. They show us how we use traditions, customs and social styles to erect high barricades to shield us from those whose ways are different from ours. In these stories we glimpse ourselves in those who depersonalize others and whom we define as types rather than as people. The city slicks and the small town hicks take on the vestments of all the "others" whom we perceive as less worthy and less right simply because they are different. Below the outer layer of these jokes lies the stern message that when we categorize people in these ways we deprive them of their humanity, in the process violating Jewish ethical teachings.

MORE JOKES ABOUT CITY SLICKS
AND SMALL TOWN HICKS

A small town Jew came to the big city and soon became ill. For a month he was confined to bed and had to pay out large sums for doctors and medicines. When he was well again, he returned to his home town and told his friends about his sojourn in the city. After describing his unanticipated illness, he added, "I'm really lucky that I took sick in the city and not here." His friends pressed him for an explanation. He said, "If I had become ill in our little town and had to spend the same amount of money for my cure, my illness would have lasted for an entire year.

—∽∼∿∾—

A hick Jew fancied himself an expert on fine music. Having never heard an opera, he traveled to the big city where a world-famous soprano was to sing the lead role in an opera. At the theatre, the cheapest ticket was ten rubles. To the Jew, this was a staggering amount to pay for a few hours of entertainment. The ticket seller advised him, "My dear man, if you really wish to see the great Elvira Pattis in today's performance, that's what you have to pay. Take my advice. It's worth it." The Jew responded, "I'm not that foolish. I didn't travel all this distance to see her. I only want to hear her."

━━∿∽━━

A young man had spent his entire life in a tiny hamlet. Now of marriageable age, he hired the services of a shad̲h̲an (marriage broker) to help him find a suitable marriage partner. The shad̲h̲an recommended a certain young woman who lived in the big city. Before setting out on the journey to meet her, the shad̲h̲an offered the young man some advice. "You will make a winning impression on the young lady if you steer your conversation with her to three topics. You must first speak to her about family. Second, you must speak to her about love. After that, you must show her how educated you are. Speak to her about philosophy. If you are successful in all three, the way to her heart will be open." Armed with this good advice, the young man set out. As soon as he was introduced to the potential bride, he asked her, "Do you have a brother?" "No," she answered. Quickly moving to the subject of love, he asked, "Do you love noodles and hot milk?" Again the answer was "no." Undeterred, he moved to the theme of philosophy. "Tell me," he said, "If you had a brother, would he love noodles and hot milk?"

━━∿∽━━

A Jew traveled from his little village to the city. On arriving, he set out to find one of his friends from home, Hershel the son of Mayer the Hebrew tutor, who had settled in the city several years earlier. It was rumored in the village that Hershel had become wealthy. Wishing to see it with his own eyes, the visitor found his way to Hershel's home. It was a palatial residence, more imposing than anything he had thought possible. "I bring you regards, Reb Hershel," he said, extending his hand to his erstwhile friend. Hershel declined to shake hands and said in a not pleasant voice, "It's time that you small town hicks learned to speak the way we do in the city. First of all, my name is no longer Reb Hershel. You are to call me Gregory Mironovich." His visitor's face reddened with embarrassment. Contritely, he corrected himself, "How are you, Gregory Mironovich?" "Quite well," the rich man answered. "In fact, extremely well. Just look about and you will see that I have been blessed with everything a person could want. This handsome house I own outright. Every morning when I awaken, my lovely daughter Raquelle serves me coffee in a demitasse. My clerk then brings me the morning mail from my office on the floor above. After I finish my coffee and have read all the mail, I go out to the veranda to rest. Then I go upstairs to my offices and give instructions to all of my secretaries. When I am done with that, I leave for a walk into town, sometimes to shop, sometimes just for the stroll. When I return, I go out to the veranda and I stretch out for a bit. In the early afternoon I have my lunch. Thank God, we eat only the finest foods. When I finish lunch, I return to the veranda for my afternoon nap. When I waken, I go to my offices to check on business matters and to give new instructions to my secretaries. From there I leave the house for a second walk into town. I return in the late afternoon in a wonderful frame of mind, and I go out to the veranda to rest for a while. This is my daily routine." The visitor was suitably awed by all that he had heard

On the first Shabbat after returning to his village, he came to the synagogue where he was immediately surrounded by all of the townsmen, all of them eager to learn if he had indeed located Hershel. "Oh yes," he said. "I found him at his home. Every rumor we have heard about him is true. He's richer than any of us can imagine. But you would never guess that he is still a Jew. He acts like a complete gentile. His listeners were aghast at his words. "Our Hershel, a Gentile? How could this be?!" He replied, "Not only Hershel, but his family too. They've all abandoned their Jewishness. Hershel is not Hershel anymore. He won't speak to you unless you call him Gregory Mironovich. His sweet little daughter isn't Rohelleh anymore. Now she is Raquelle. And Bryna who was always such a proper and modest Jewish wife, she isn't Bryna anymore. Her name is now veranda."

⎯⎯∿∿⎯⎯

Back home after a visit to the city, a shtetl Jew was describing to his friends the wonders and miracles he had seen there. He exclaimed, "You've never seen anything like the hotels they have there. One is more elegant than the next. In my hotel, for example, you can sit in your room and if you feel like having a cup of coffee, you don't have to leave the room. All you do is press a button on a panel near your bed. Before you know it, there's a knock at your door. You open it and a maid enters carrying a cup of steaming coffee." "Oh my," exclaimed one of his listeners, "if only you had brought back one of those buttons!"

JEW AGAINST JEW

A tale is told of a Jew, the sole survivor of a shipwreck. Washed ashore on a deserted island, he lived alone for many years. When at last he was found, he proudly showed his rescuers the three buildings he had built during his years of isolation. One was his home. The second, adorned with a six-pointed Star of David was his synagogue. The third building was an identical replica of the second. One of his rescuers asked, "Why do you have two synagogues?" "Oh" he answered, pointing to the second one, "That one is the one I don't go to."

Most Jews whether at home in a synagogue or not will laugh at this story because it is a play on a familiar truism; namely that Jews are contentious. Jewish history is peppered with religious disagreements and ideological quarrels with far-reaching consequences. Disputations between Jew and Jew are rife and begin with the Bible. The original State of Israel, the monarchy established by King Saul, broke apart after the death of King Solomon, and re-emerged as two separate kingdoms marked by fierce enmity between them. The Dead Sea Scrolls, discovered in the Twentieth Century, revealed that more than two thousand years ago, disaffected Jews began to abandon Jerusalem and other cities. They could not abide the teachings and practices of the entrenched religious leadership so they created separatist communities. Not long after, another fateful fracture occurred in Israel between the Sadducees and the Pharisees over how to interpret the Torah. The birth of Christianity during the same period when seen as an event within Judaism can be regarded as the outcome of yet another internal struggle among Jews over the path to redemption. Centuries later, another struggle broke apart Jewish communities in many parts of the world. Great numbers of Jews rallied to the call of Kara'ism, rejecting all rabbinic interpretation of Torah, accepting only the literal word of the Torah as binding. Kara'ite communities emerged in the Middle East, in North Africa and in Europe, some of them continuing to exist to the present time, despite being ostracized by mainstream Jewry, followers of rabbinic law.

Still another fierce conflict erupted between Jews who integrated philosophical and scientific truths into traditional Jewish faith and those who vehemently opposed all knowledge external to the Torah.

This "war of knowledge" alternately sputtered or burned like a fierce fire, and even now continues to divide Jews.

The Jewish revivalist movement known as Hassidism met with fierce opposition of the Mitnagdim (the name means "the opposition party"). For generations anti-Hassidic rabbis competed with each other in issuing public bans forbidding contact between Mitnagdim and Hassidim. They declared Hassidic synagogues off-limits, forbidding Jews to pray in them because of their divergent prayer customs. They harshly discouraged even ordinary social contacts between the two groups. Small wonder that the tale of the shipwrecked Jew virtually guarantees Jewish laughter.

Internal conflict is, of course, one of the primary spawning grounds of humor. Jews found in it exceptionally fertile material for the humor of ridicule. In Jew against Jew the focus is on the bitter disputes between Hassidim and Mitnagdim as one example in the long history of polarizing confrontations among Jews.

The Hassidic rebbe, adored and idolized by his followers, frequently brought a unique emotional fervor into religious experience, especially in the realm of prayer, far beyond what Jews had previously known. Many of Hassidism's core doctrines came from older mystical teachings of the Kabbalah. What had once been the esoteric possession of a privileged few was reworked by Hassidic teachers into the everyday discourse of the masses. Hassidism introduced another novel feature, the belief in the rebbe as a miracle-worker.

These behaviors and doctrines antagonized the traditionalists who utilized humor as one of their weapons against their ideological foes. There is no end to jokes which portray the rebbe as both buffoon and ignoramus, unfit to lead a community. The rebbe's teachings are held up to ridicule and reviled as the rejection of the heritage of true Torah study. In the hands of the Mitnagdim, whose ranks included both religious and secular Jews, anti-Hassidic humor was a weapon of open warfare. They lampooned the rebbe as a fraudulent teacher of Judaism. These jokes were part of a massive effort to discredit Hassidism. They are not the polite living-room variety of jokes. They were openly vituperative, and deliberately crossed the line that separates playful humor from willful character assassination.

Our first two examples are typical of the genre.

The aged rebbe, of blessed memory, was once on a journey, escorted by several of his most devoted disciples. One evening, they stopped at an inn where they hoped to spend the night. The inn-keeper was a fellow Jew who had little regard for Hassidim. He disdained the rebbe, nor did he offer him or his followers lodgings for the night. Deeply angered and humiliated by this show of disrespect, the rebbe called out in a loud, solemn voice, quivering with emotion, "From heaven above, I call down a curse upon the pillar that supports the roof of this inn. This pillar which has been denied the honor of having a Tzaddik of the Lord spend the night in its presence shall be turned into a poisonous snake, and the entire inn shall crash to the ground!" The inn-keeper and his wife, hearing the rebbe's dreadful curse fell to the ground, prostrating themselves at his feet, and weeping. They begged him to rescind the curse and to spare them and the inn. Their remorse filled the rebbe with compassion. He raised his eyes heavenward and called out a second time, "O Lord, I shall overlook the great indignity I have suffered. May it be Your will also, O Lord, to overlook the curse I have called down upon this place. Let the pillar remain as it is." The rebbe's prayer was answered, and ever since that time, the story has been told far and near, and people have come from the ends of the earth to visit the inn and to gaze in wonder upon the pillar which remained unchanged because of the rebbe's great mercy.

—∿∿∿—

A Mitnaged happened to be sitting with a group of Hassidim, listening with disbelief as they told tales of the wonders and miracles their rebbes had performed. Unable to restrain himself, he said to them, "Such nonsense you believe! Not one of you saw those things with your own eyes. There's not a kernel of truth in any of those tales. But I will tell you about something miraculous that I saw with my own eyes. You should know that I am opposed to everything you believe about your rebbes, but even so, there was once an occasion when I paid a visit to a rebbe to seek his advice. I found the door to his study locked, and I was told that I could not enter until he himself would unlock the door for me. I could not resist my curiosity, and for one entire hour I crouched by the key-hole and peered into the rebbe's room. I saw him wash his hands and recite the blessing with the most intense concentration. I saw him recite the blessing for bread with the same concentration. I watched as he dipped a piece of the bread into salt before taking a bite. I saw his servant place before him a platter with a stuffed chicken. I watched in awe as he gazed at the chicken, and, in a flash, I saw it turned into a pile of bones."

Both stories have one goal; to expose rebbes as manipulators and misleaders of the naïve followers who flocked to them. Their subtext is that nothing can be more pathetic than the sight of religious Jews who allow themselves to be so easily duped. The two jokes are a denunciation of Jews who suspend their critical judgment and avidly credit the rebbes with the power to create miracles even where no miracles have occurred. There is a further repudiation in these stories. Judaism, unlike Christianity, had never before claimed for its clergy the role of the indispensable conduit connecting the ordinary Jew with God. Hassidism broke new ground and claimed this role for its rebbes, setting in motion a major ideological shift fraught with enormous consequences. The two opposing sides, Hassidim and Mitnagdim, became so polarized that reasoned debate between them was not possible. Many jokes took aim at all aspects of the Hassidic way to God, and thus are a commentary on this bitter internal struggle for the souls of Jews. The majority of jokes in this genre are anti-Hassidic.

MORE JOKES ABOUT JEWS AGAINST JEWS

A Hassid told the following story. "We were gathered in the holy presence of our saintly rebbe in Rahmistrovka. We were drinking in every one of his holy teachings. Suddenly he leaped from his chair, and a dreadful groan burst from his mouth. In agony he cried out, "A fire! A horrible fire from heaven!" We sat mesmerized with shock and fright. A moment later, the rebbe collapsed in his chair, tears streaming from his eyes, sobbing in anguish, "Lishtshin, Oy, Lishtshin! It's on fire.! The whole town is burning up in flames."

Those who heard the Hassid tell the story were stunned into silence, until one of them asked, "Was there really a fire in Lishtshin at that very moment?" The Hassid answered, "No. There was no fire at all." His listeners sat bewildered, and again one of them asked, "If there was no fire, what kind of a miracle did your rebbe perform? He responded, "I never said it was a miracle, but you have to admit that for the rebbe to be able to see all the way from Rahmistrovka to Lishtshin, that's really something!

꞊꜠꜠꜡꜡꜡

A group of Hassidim were gathered in a roadside inn. They spent the evening regaling themselves with stories of the wondrous powers of their rebbes. One told the following tale, "It happened one summer that the sun unleashed a blazing heat, so intense that it turned the town's river into a mud hole. The pious Jewish wives of the town confronted the rebbe with their tale of woe, "Rebbe, what shall we do? The river is practically dry. Where shall we find fish for the Sabbath?" Immediately, the rebbe put away his holy books, strode from his house, and marched to the edge of the river. Stretching out his arms, and lifting his eyes toward heaven, he proclaimed, "River, river, I demand that you send up fish from your depths!" The housewives watched intently; suddenly a fish wiggled free from the

mud, leaped into the air and landed at the rebbe's feet. A second later it was followed by another fish. In a flash five more
came, then ten more, twenty more, a hundred more. It was a
sight to behold. In less time than it takes to tell the story, a
mountain of thousands of fish was piled up at the feet of our
saintly rebbe.

A second Hassid, not to be outdone, spoke up, "Indeed, that
was a true miracle, but a small one compared to what I once
saw with my own eyes. In our town, the rain began to fall right
after Yom Kippur. At first we greeted it as a blessing, but soon
it turned into a deluge that would not stop. Day after day it fell
without end. The sky in the daytime was as dark as on the
darkest night. On the evening when special prayers were to be
said to greet the new moon, we gathered out of doors, the storm
clouds had obliterated the heavens. There was no new moon to
be seen. All eyes turned to the rebbe, and we appealed to him,
"Rebbe, your people want to say the prayer to greet the new
moon, but there is no moon to be seen." Without a moment's
delay, the rebbe did a remarkable thing. He removed the gartel
(the prayer sash) from around his waist, stretched it taut with
both hands and held it high above his head and in a loud voice
called out, "I demand O heavens that the new moon appear!"
Suddenly a crack seemed to appear in the sky. The heavens
opened and the tiny sliver of the new moon began to emerge.
A cheer went up from all of us as the new moon began to cast
its bright light over our heads. A moment later we were si-
lenced and awe-struck as we watched a second moon appear,
then a third, then five more, then fifty.... and so many more
that we could not count them!"

During an evening gathering when the drinks were flowing
freely, Jews were trading stories about their rebbes and their
miracles. One related, "My rebbe was once on a journey accompanied by members of his family. It was a Friday and they

were headed to a town a considerable distance from their own. Many miles before reaching their destination a mishap occurred; a wheel of their wagon came off. It took several hours for the coachman to make the repair, and by this time it was too late to reach their destination before the arrival of Shabbat. The sun was beginning to dip low in the sky; the shadows of evening were coming closer. The holy Sabbath had arrived, and it was now forbidden to travel. At that moment the rebbe began to pray and a miracle occurred. To the right of the road there was darkness. To the left of the road there was darkness. The rebbe's coach traveled straight down the center where the sky was bright with light.

⸻

A Hassid related, "The rebbe's journey took him through an unfriendly village. Hooligans lined the sides of the road and made ready to pelt his carriage with stones. Unafraid, the rebbe recited aloud a verse from the Torah, "The might of Your arm shall make them rigid as stone" (Exodus 15)." Immediately the arms of his would-be attackers became paralyzed. A listener to the story reacted in great surprise, "If that's the case, why did your rebbe return home with a swollen eye?" The Hassid explained, "One of the hooligans was hard of hearing."

⸻

A group of disciples sat and related tales of miracles their rebbes had performed. With each telling, the stories grew more and more extreme, until one of them blurted out, "All the stories you are telling are nothing but hearsay. You didn't witness the deeds yourselves. Let me tell you about an incredible event I witnessed with my own eyes. It happened last summer. One of our fellow Jews walked out of his home hale, hearty and in full vigor. Suddenly he lurched forward and fell stricken to the ground. I myself ran to summon the rebbe, long may he live. I told him what had happened. He ran to the lifeless man

*and placed his hands on his head. I heard him speak into his ear,
"I command you, rise up, rise up!" One of the listeners asked,
"Did he rise up?" "No," came the response, "he did not rise
up, he was dead." His listeners hooted in derision, "What kind
of miracle is that supposed to be?" He replied, "A miracle, I
don't know.... But I was present; I saw it with my own eyes!"*

———◈◈———

*The old rebbe died, and in the fashion of Hassidic custom, his
very young son succeeded him as head of the community. Soon
after, a group of disciples came to him and begged for his in-
tercession to end the drought and bring rain. The new rebbe
did as he was asked and his prayers were answered. The rain
came, but unfortunately the heavens would not close. For days
and days the rains poured down. The streets were impassable,
homes were flooded, life had turned miserable. The same disciples came to the rebbe again and urgently pleaded for another
miracle. They begged him to intercede once more with God so
that the rains would stop. Again he did as requested; he prayed,
but the rains did not stop. The rebbe's assistant explained to the
disappointed disciples, "Our rebbe is still very inexperienced.
He knows how to start the rain, but he hasn't learned yet how
to make it stop."*

———◈◈———

*No Hassid brought a personal request to a rebbe without leav-
ing a monetary gift in appreciation, called a "pidyon." It was
the custom to leave the pidyon with the rebbe's assistant. A
lumber merchant came once to his rebbe with a special request,
but first he left with the assistant three hundred thirty three
gold pieces, equal to the numerical value of the Hebrew word
"sheleg" (snow). The Hassid was admitted to the rebbe's presence and implored him to use his miraculous powers to cause
a snow storm that would make all the roads slippery. This
would ease the burden for his horses as they pulled the tree*

*trunks from the forest to the saw mill. The rebbe assured him
that he would intercede with God to send snow. The lumber
merchant left filled with optimism. Several days later he returned with a complaint, "Rebbe, you prayed for snow, but
since I saw you it has been raining non-stop. There isn't a sign
of snow." The rebbe looked at him sternly and shook his head,
"I prayed for the miracle you wanted, and then I learned that
you also gave my assistant a personal gift of ten gold coins.
That spoiled everything. You didn't realize that with your gift
to my assistant you increased the numerical value to that of
"geshem"* (the Hebrew word for rain; its letters add up to
three hundred forty three).

꠵ꞏꞏꞏꞏ꠵

*The wife of a <u>H</u>assid was gravely ill. Her doctor had given up
all hope for a recovery. Her husband wasted no time. He rushed
to the rebbe and implored him to perform a miracle and save
her life. The rebbe entered his private room and spent many
minutes in solitary prayer. When he emerged, his face was
beaming. He announced to the husband, "I have wrestled with
the angel of death until I succeeded in wrenching the sword
from his grasp. Your wife is now safe and well. Go home and
rejoice with her and with your children." Overjoyed, his heart
bursting with happiness, the man raced home where he found
his children weeping bitterly, "Father, our mother is dead!"
The <u>H</u>assid groaned and cried out in his grief, "O that terrible
angel of death. He must have choked her with his hands."*

꠵ꞏꞏꞏꞏ꠵

*The Mitnagdim let no opportunity pass to mock and humili-
ate their opponents, the <u>H</u>assidim. A Mitnaged once found
himself in the presence of a group of <u>H</u>assidim. He grew tired
of hearing their tales. Scornfully he said to them, "All these
miracles you talk about; they're nothing but made up stories.
There isn't an ounce of truth in them. They never happened."*

One Hassid answered in anger, "You are nothing but a foolish Mitnaged. You are the one who doesn't know what he's talking about. We Hassidim know that miracles can happen at any moment. I myself had the privilege of witnessing my rebbe per-form a miracle. I was present when he, may his name be a bless-ing, went into his private chamber to meditate. I could not contain my curiosity. He was so deep in concentration that he neither heard nor saw me when I entered his room. I stood in a corner away from his eyes and watched. I saw the rebbe sit-ting at his table. His eyes were shut and his face was drained of color. Never had I seen him so pale. I gazed as he opened his eyes and reached for a bottle of red wine standing on the table. I saw him open the bottle and fill a glass with wine. I watched as he slowly lifted the glass to his lips and drink the wine. I watched in awe as he did this again and again until there was nothing left in the bottle. What I saw next was beyond belief. The rebbe's face, which had been as pale as the face of a ghost, had turned as red as a beet, and the wine bottle was now com-pletely without color.

━∿∿━

One Hassid asked another, "What would we do if, God forbid, money suddenly ceased to exist? What gifts would we be able to bring to our Rebbes?" The other Hassid answered, "Such a fool you are. If money, God forbid, did not exist, there would be no Rebbes either."

━∿∿━

Three Hassidim chanced to meet at an inn. Naturally, their conversation turned to stories about their rebbes. The first one said, "My rebbe, long may he live, is so meticulous about ob-serving our dietary laws that he insists on having two cooks in his home; one to prepare all the meat meals, and one to prepare all the dairy meals." The second one said, "My rebbe, long may he live, is even stricter. If he eats meat, he doesn't wait the cus-

tomary six hours before tasting anything dairy. He waits an entire day." The third Hassid, not to be outdone by the first two, said, "My rebbe, long may he live, is even stricter than that. If he is studying in the holy books the chapters concerning the preparation of meat dishes, he waits a full day before turning to the chapters about dairy foods.

⎯⎯∿∿⎯⎯

Several Hassidim were boasting to each other about the great piety of their rebbes. One said, "When my rebbe sets out on a journey, he takes with him his own cantor and ritual slaughterer. The second one said, "My rebbe does the same, but he goes even further. He takes with him his own scroll of the Torah. The third Hassid outdid the others. He said, "My rebbe is so strict that when he starts out on a journey, he brings with him his cantor and ritual slaughter, his scroll of the Torah, and he also takes along his own "mikveh" (ritual bathing pool).

⎯⎯∿∿⎯⎯

The rebbe was relaxing in his private chamber, bantering with his assistant. He asked him, "Do you ever imagine that you could be a Rebbe like me?" The assistant answered, "Yes, rebbe, I have given thought to that. I know that I could be like you in every respect but one." The rebbe, his curiosity aroused, inquired, "And what would that be?" The assistant paused, choosing his words carefully, "I would be able to imitate the way you groan with sympathy whenever Hassidim seek your help to beg for a miracle. I know that I could imitate the way you pray for barren women to conceive a child, or how you pray for the sick to be healed. All these I have learned by watching what you do. But I have also seen you every evening; how you carefully count every last penny your followers give you, and how you sweep them off the table into your pocket without a trace of a smile on your face. This is something that I would not be able to imitate."

⟨≈⟩

*A Hassid related with great pride this story about his rebbe,
"All day long he busies himself with the study of our holy
books. All night long he devotes himself to the needs of his followers." A listener asked, "If that's the case, when does your
rebbe sleep?" He replied, "Our rebbe sleeps for only one hour,
just before the morning prayers." "But," his questioner continued, "How can he manage on only one hour of sleep?" The
proud Hassid responded, "My rebbe is a great maker of miracles. He can sleep more in one hour than someone who sleeps
the whole night."*

⟨≈⟩

*A Mitnaged entered the rebbe's private chamber. He found the
rebbe seated at his table, a steaming plate piled high with juicy
pancakes in front of him. He saw the rebbe take a salt shaker
and empty it over the pancakes. The Mitnaged could not
fathom the rebbe's strange behavior. The rebbe's assistant explained to him, "The rebbe does this so as not to enjoy the pancakes. In this way he protects himself from indulging in the
pleasures of this world. As the assistant was escorting the Mitnaged from the rebbe's home, he noticed the rebbe's wife, an at-
tractive woman, tastefully clothed, and adorned with elegant
jewelry. He whispered to the rebbe's assistant, "I wonder how
much salt he pours on her."*

⟨≈⟩

*A Mitnaged rabbi, a life-long opponent of Hassidism, had an
even greater disdain for the men who became rebbes. He liked
to say, "Anyone can walk around in a disguise. With the right
clothing you can pretend to be a general of the army and people will believe you. But no one can disguise himself and pretend to be a Hassidic rebbe. The moment you place a rebbe's*

hat on your head and wear a rebbe's silk garments, and hire an assistant to collect contributions for you, you are no longer pretending. At that moment you are a real rebbe!"

⸺∿∿⸺

A famous rebbe visited the town of Shedlitz. News of his arrival spread quickly throughout the town. Hordes of people came to the inn where he was staying, bringing their contributions and seeking his blessings. The town's official rabbi, an opponent of the Hassidim, was among those who came to call on the rebbe. The latter was overjoyed, his pride and ego swelling at the thought that so distinguished a personage would come to meet with him. Adopting his most humble tone of voice, the rebbe asked, "Why have you troubled yourself to call upon me?" The rabbi replied, "I wanted to see with my own eyes how a sup-posedly God-fearing Jew takes money for nothing."

⸺∿∿⸺

A Hassid met with a rabbi who had low regard for Hassidim and their rebbes. The Hassid boasted to him of the many af-flictions he had taken upon himself in order to elevate his soul by denying himself pleasures of this world. He said, "I do not imbibe any drink other than water. My shoes have pointy nails sticking into the soles of my feet. In the winter I roll in the snow. Daily I submit myself to lashes from the whip." The Rabbi pointed a finger to the window and said, "Look out there to the meadow. Do you see who is there? He too drinks only water. He too has nails sticking up from his shoes and piercing his feet. He too rolls in the snow and receives daily lashes from the whip. In spite of all this, he remains a "ferd" (Yiddish for horse; colloquially, a fool).

⸺∿∿⸺

Some Mitnagdim were engaged in their favorite past-time, sharing stories that belittled the town's Hassidic rebbe. Sitting nearby was one of the rebbe's followers. He jumped to his feet and shouted, "Unworthy Jews, each of you! May you have sand poured into your mouths for your blasphemies! How dare you malign a person who is so holy that he receives a personal revelation from the Prophet Elijah every Friday just before the Sabbath?!" A Mitnaged challenged him, "How do you know that he receives such revelations?" The Hassid answered, "I heard it myself from the rebbe's sainted lips." The Mitnaged did not back down, "Perhaps the rebbe was telling you a false-hood?" The Hassid was aghast at the thought. He retorted in anger, "Would a person who receives revelations from the Prophet Elijah have to tell a lie?!"

⸺⸻⸺

The final two stories reverse the equation. In these tales, representative of the relatively few jokes in which Mitnagdim are put to shame, Hassidim emerge the victors.

A wonder-working rebbe came to town. Day after day, from early morning until late at night, Jews stood in line waiting to have an audience with him, hoping to obtain miraculous cures or escape from every kind of misfortune. Among them was a skeptic, altogether a non-believer when it came to miracle-mak-ing rebbes. He proclaimed to the others who waited in line, "Fellow Jews, I shall expose him to you as a faker, and he will be powerless to harm me." He approached the rebbe and said, "O exalted rebbe, I beseech you to perform a miracle on my be-half and rid me of the three terrible afflictions that give me no peace." The wonder-worker gazed deeply into the man's eyes and sensed that he was not a true believer. He asked, "What are the afflictions that are causing you so much misery?" The skeptic replied, "Sickness has robbed me of my sense of taste; it has stolen from me my ability to tell the truth, and it has erased my memory." The rebbe said to him, "I shall work a miracle for you. I will cure you of all three of your ills." The rebbe took something from his bag and commanded the skeptic, "Open wide your mouth." The man did as directed. The rebbe quickly put into the man's mouth an object he had taken from his bag. In a second the skeptic's body began to convulse. With a terrible noise, he spat out the object. "What horrible garbage," he screamed. The wonder-worker rebbe smiled and replied, "You are now cured. You came to me a sick man, and now you are well. You have gotten back your sense of taste, you spoke the truth, and you had no difficulty remembering that I placed a piece of foul garbage in your mouth."

⟞∿∿⟝

A rebbe and a Mitnaged chanced to be fellow passengers on the same train. They shared adjacent seats in the third-class coach. The Mitnaged wasted no time in disparaging the rebbe. With mock astonishment he said, "I'm amazed that a person as great and righteous as you deigns to travel in third-class among the most common mortals!" The rebbe heaved a sigh and responded, "Not all rebbes are of equal worth. Some indeed have risen to the highest level of righteousness, and some are still at the lowest level. I am still a third-class rebbe. I know my place; this is where I belong. But you are indeed a first-class person. Your impudence, your brazenness and your vulgarity are of the highest order. How do you explain that you are sitting in third-class with people like me?!"

TO TELL THE TRUTH

Mark Twain is remembered for many trenchant observations about human failings; among them his tongue-in-cheek advice, "When in doubt, tell the truth." This kind of wry comment makes us nod our heads knowingly. Telling the truth is a self-evident expectation; unfortunately it is also one of the most problematic. The first Jewish articulation on truth found in the Torah warns, "Keep distant from falsehood" (Exodus 23:17). This terse order allows for no doubt that we are dealing with anything but an absolute command. Truth telling, in Judaism, is a bed-rock foundation of an ethical life. It is non-negotiable; it allows for no compromise. The problem, of course, with the Torah's stern command is that it also allows no wiggle room.

Everyday experience confirms for us in a thousand different ways that total honesty is unattainable. For most of us, truth works like a rubber-band; to be stretched and contracted. Talmudic discussions about truth recognize the rigidity of the Torah's approach. The Sages held firmly to the ideal of honesty in speech and in deed, but allowed for one single exception. They provided for leniency in one sensitive area of human relationships, the words between a husband and wife. They accepted telling a "white lie" as ethical if it serves the single purpose of helping to sustain a marital relationship. Maintaining harmony between marital partners (in Hebrew, *shlohm bayit*) was deemed sufficient justification to stretch the truth.

I have no doubt that falsehood in all its forms is the most frequently practiced breach of ethics in daily life. Why then does Jewish ethical teaching, with the exception noted above, hold us to such an unyielding standard? My late teacher, Rabbi Louis Finkelstein – for many years Chancellor of The Jewish Theological Seminary of America – was fond of saying that Judaism expects of ordinary Jews what other religions ask only of their saints. The Torah's goal is that all Jews become saints, however unreasonable that may seem.

Untruths come in different guises, and they can be easily classified, whether as outright lies, misrepresentation, deception, innuendo, or malevolent rumor-mongering. In each case, one of the parties is duped into believing that the message is true. Other forms of speech, such as deliberate omission of important facts, even excessive flattery, are less severe than an outright lie, but may also be unacceptable when their primary aim is to cause loss or harm.

A word has to be added about a type of untruth which may or may not be malicious in its intent, the use of exaggeration. Tellers of Jewish jokes love anecdotes built on exaggeration. It is highly likely that some of these originated in non-Jewish sources and then underwent a thorough "koshering" process. In Jewish exaggeration jokes, we find two general types; one serious, the other playful. The serious ones portray the harm we create through flagrant exaggeration, whereas playful exaggeration is considered benign hyperbole intended to simply amuse.

Our first anecdote is based on an outright deception where the goal is personal gain at another's expense. The second is typical of stories built upon fantasies where there is no intent to cause hurt.

The father of Simon and Levi had died. The two sons were embroiled in controversy, each contending that their father intended that he should receive the major part of the estate. They hired attorneys and took the matter to court. On the evening before the judge was to hear the case, Simon confided to his attorney that he was planning to send a substantial sum of money to the judge to influence his decision. The attorney could barely restrain his shock, "If you do such a thing, the judge will consider you a conniver and the worst kind of thief. He will declare your brother the winner, and you will be charged with attempted bribery!" The next day the judge heard the case and ruled in favor of Simon. As they left the court, Simon's attorney said to him, "I'm glad that you took my advice. Otherwise you would have not won." Simon chuckled, "It's a good thing that I didn't listen to you. I sent the gift to the judge, but I signed my brother's name to it."

⟞∿∾⟝

You say you don't believe in miracles? Let me tell you about a miracle that happened to me. It was during the winter. No one could recall a winter as cold as that one. Everything was frozen solid. The river had turned into a block of ice. A team of horses pulling the biggest wagon, loaded with the heaviest merchandise, could travel safer and faster on the frozen river than on the road. One day I was crossing the river on foot. I had nearly reached the opposite bank when suddenly there was a sound like thunder. A huge crack opened in the ice and I fell into the frigid water. I screamed for help. Two peasants heard my cries. They rushed onto the ice, pulled me from the water and dragged me to the shore. I was like a block of ice myself. My entire body, my beard and my clothing, were one frozen mass. My rescuers carried me to their house, a tiny hovel that didn't have a scrap of food in it. That's how poor they were. They stood me near the fire place, and slowly the heat began to thaw me out. Two large fish that had been trapped in my beard fell to the floor and began flapping. It was a double miracle. My life had been saved, and I was able to provide a meal for my rescuers.

—⁓⁓—

If the first joke made you laugh, you are probably not alone. In the classic tradition of good jokes, this one cleverly sets us up for the unexpected punch line. If you also thought that it is a despicable tale and an indictment of an ethical breach, you are hopefully one of a large company of people. It should not surprise us that where money is involved, even ties of blood are not strong enough to deter some people from victimizing close family members. The point of the story is that greed wins the prize.

The second story is a delightful contrast. Here too truth is sacrificed, but not for personal gain, and certainly not to harm another person. This is a story in which no one is being manipulated and no one is tricked. Best of all, no one is a loser. At the end of the story everyone is grateful. It is a useful counter-point to the first story. In the story of the two brothers, selfishness leads inexorably to aggression. Its main ethical lesson is that greed is never self-contained. It demands a target, and once successful its appetite grows and the scale of aggression expands.

LIARS, FAST TALKERS, DECEIVERS AND MANIPULATORS

A child asked his father, "Can you explain to me what a conscience problem is?" The father replied, "I'll give you an example. If a customer comes into my store and buys something for one dollar, and by mistake gives me three dollars, I suddenly have a conscience problem – do I tell my partner or not?"

⤳⤳〰〰

A merchant, known for his shady practices, sold a colored garment to a gullible woman. When she arrived home and unwrapped her package, she discovered a white garment inside. She returned to the store and accused the merchant of deceiving her. He insisted that he had done no such thing. She sued him in court where the judge agreed with her complaint. The merchant protested his innocence. He claimed that he had in fact sold her a colored garment, but that it had somehow lost its color. The incredulous judge demanded an explanation. The merchant said, "It's the nature of certain goods to lose their color." He offered himself as an example, saying, "Look at my beard; originally it was black, but now it's all white.

⤳⤳〰〰

Three friends, a priest, a pastor and a rabbi, celebrated the twenty fifth anniversary of their weekly card game by booking passage on a cruise ship. They were well aware that the ship's captain forbade all forms of gambling on board the vessel. Undeterred, the three clergymen passed their time at sea gambling in their stateroom. Word reached the captain who summoned them to his quarters. "It's been reported to me that you have been gambling," he said to them. Eying the priest, he said in a stern voice, "Father, you surely would not tell an untruth. Were you gambling?" The priest denied that he had been gambling. The captain turned to the pastor, "I know that you are an honorable man of the Lord and will not lie, "Were you and the others gambling?" The pastor calmly denied that any gambling had occurred. Turning to the last of the three men, the captain continued, "Rabbi, surely you would not speak a falsehood. Were you gambling?" With a look of innocence, the rabbi answered, "With whom?"

———

A Jew faced charges of counterfeiting an expensive brand of perfume. At his trial, the judge asked him if he was prepared to confess to the crime. The accused refused to confess. The judge admonished him, "Surely you must understand that the counterfeit perfume found in your work-shop is clear evidence of your guilt. We have with us a chemist who is a recognized expert, and he is prepared to testify to the court that the perfume you had in your possession was indeed counterfeit." The accused responded, "Your honor, will you grant me permission to address a question to the bench?" The judge granted the request. The accused asked, "Your honor, are you an expert in chemistry?" The judge replied, "My field is the law. I know nothing about chemistry. That is why we have an expert chemist who is ready to testify." The accused turned to the chemist and asked, "Are you, sir, expert in matters of law?" The chemist replied, "I know nothing about jurisprudence. His honor, the judge, is the expert in matters of law." At this the accused addressed the judge. "Your honor," he said, "it is obvious that each of you is a specialist, yet you, the judge, know nothing about chemistry, and he, the chemist, knows nothing about the law. Here I am, a simple Jew with only minimal education. Is it reasonable that I should be expected to be expert in both chemistry and the law?"

———

A certain rabbi was often heard to say that a liar is a worse sinner than every kind of thief. There is one kind of thief, he explained, who breaks in only at night. Another kind enters in broad daylight. Some thieves take only from one person at a time, while others know how to defraud an entire class of people at the same time. But a liar makes no distinctions. He's at work by day and by night. It makes no difference to him whether he tricks one person or many.

≈≈≈≈≈

A man told a story that seemed beyond belief. None of the listeners thought it could possibly be true. He said to them, "If you don't believe me, go ask the rabbi. He was there when it happened." They went to the rabbi. He heard their account and said to them, "I'm in awe of that man's memory. I have known people who can remember every detail of something that happened twenty years ago. I've even known some who can recall exactly what occurred fifty years ago. But this man is in a class by himself. He can remember things that never happened!"

≈≈≈≈≈

An old man and a young man were partners in a business. A dispute broke out between them, and they went to a lawyer to seek help in resolving it. The younger man immediately began to recite to the lawyer his version of the disagreement. The older man interrupted, "Take my advice; stick to the facts and leave it to the lawyer to add all the lies."

≈≈≈≈≈

A group of people wagered with a notorious liar that they could trip him up in an untruth. They said, "We'll give you a hundred dollars on condition that you tell a lie. He responded, "I would gladly take the hundred dollars, but I am sorry to say that I cannot meet the condition. In my entire life, I have never told a lie."

≈≈≈≈≈

FANTASTIC TALES & HARMLESS EXAGGERATORS

A hiker came across an enormous apple tree whose upper branches reached into the clouds. Gazing upward, he saw ripe apples. After hours of climbing, he reached the apples. Never had he seen such gigantic ones. They were so large that he barely had room for three of them in his knapsack. Climbing back down, he paused to eat one of them. Biting into the huge apple, a seed fell out, and many seconds later it hit the ground with a thunderous noise. The impact was so great that it gouged a deep crater into the earth.

≈∿∿≈

A poor Jew had been reduced to begging for alms. In the course of conversation with a kindly benefactor, he boasted to him that he hadn't always been poor. He said, "My family was so wealthy, my mother had earrings made of gold. They weighed ten pounds." His astonished patron exclaimed, "Ten pounds? How could that possibly be? Surely they would have torn her ear-lobes!" The beggar explained, "The earrings were hollow."

≈∿∿≈

It was only hours until the start of the Passover holiday. In the house there was not a sign of anything needed for the Seder ceremony. There was no wine, no matzos, no potatoes, not an apple or an egg. Nothing. The distraught wife was in tears. The children looked hopelessly forlorn. The sad husband wandered aimlessly in the market place, praying for a miracle. Suddenly the horse and carriage of the town's wealthiest aristocrat entered the market area and came to a stop alongside the poor man. A footman descended from the carriage, opened the door and assisted the aristocrat's wife as she stepped down to the street. The poor man stood there and gaped in awe. He was also the only one to notice that her handkerchief had fallen to the ground. He retrieved it and found inside the answer to his prayer, fifty gold coins together with a grandfather clock.

———∞∾∾———

A group of drinkers sat in the tavern and shared stories. One recounted a hair-raising escape he had experienced. "I was walking alone in the thickest part of the forest when suddenly I was surrounded by ninety nine snarling, ferocious wolves. They moved closer and closer, preparing to attack. One of his listeners reacted with great skepticism. He asked," You were surrounded by hungry wolves and yet you were able to tell that there were ninety nine of them?" The story-teller explained, "The truth is that there were actually one hundred of them, but I was afraid that if I said one hundred, you would think that I was exaggerating."

The same drinkers listened as another one told of his own narrow escape from disaster. "I too was all alone in the forest. I heard a noise, and suddenly I was being menaced by one hundred wolves. I think it was a hundred, but for sure there were at least fifty." A listener shook his head in disbelief, "Are you sure it wasn't closer to twenty?" Unruffled, the story-teller replied, "Are you doubting my word? Even if it had been only a single wolf, I would have been in terrible danger." Another listener chimed in, "Are you sure it was a wolf you saw?" Not disturbed in the least, the story-teller concluded his tale, "If it wasn't a wolf, what else could have been making that noise in the forest?"

———∞∾∾———

Jews were assembled in the prayer house waiting for the evening service to begin. One of them related how he had been out for a stroll earlier that same day and passed the home of an unfriendly person who kept a ferocious dog. Suddenly the dog leaped over the fence and barred his way. "The dog," he said, "was gigantic, more like a lion than a dog. If I hadn't had my wits about me, the dog would have torn me to pieces. At the moment the dog was about to pounce on me, he opened wide his mouth. I grabbed hold of his tongue, and with all my might I dragged him after me. I pulled his tongue with such force that I turned the dog inside out." His listeners sat in astonished silence. Finally one of them asked, "Is that the end of the story?" "There is more," the man acknowledged; "the dog barks now from his rear end."

———∿∿∿∿———

One Russian Jew speaks to another, "Let me tell you about winters in Moscow. You can't imagine the cold we have. One day I walked out to the street. The cold was unbearable. I had to clear my throat, but before the spittle reached the ground, it was frozen into a small stone." His friend smiled, but remained unimpressed. "You call that cold! Let me tell you about winter in Siberia. I was in Irkutsk. I met a man in the market and we began to converse. As the words came out of my mouth, they turned to ice. We were able to read them before they hit the ground."

———∿∿∿∿———

A visitor to America returned to his village in Poland. His family and friends gathered around him and listened, mouths opened wide in disbelief, as he told them wondrous tales of all he had seen. "Have you heard about skyscrapers," he asked them. "In New York I climbed the tallest one. It took me days and nights until I reached the top. I had to crawl on my belly to keep from bumping my head on the moon."

———∿∿∿∿———

Do you want to know how thick the fog is in London? A friend and I were walking down a London street. Out of nowhere a fly flew into my nose. I took a handkerchief from my pocket to blow my nose. Just at that moment a thick blanket of fog descended over London. The city turned so black, I couldn't see a thing. By mistake I blew my friend's nose."

꘎꘎

One friend told another, "Yesterday I went to the museum. They had on exhibit the hammer that Cain used to slay his brother." Not to be outdone, his friend responded, "That's nothing. Last week the museum exhibited the ladder Jacob saw in his dream."

꘎꘎

A wealthy customer was examining antique wrist watches in a fancy jewelry store. The shop-keeper pointed to one in particular. "This is a rare piece," he said. "You won't find its equal anywhere in the world. It was originally owned by Maimonides, the great physician who was also a famous philosopher. He used this watch when he took the pulse of his patients. He brought it with him when he moved from Egypt to America." The customer was amazed. "How can that be? Maimonides lived in the twelfth century before watches were invented, and before anyone knew about America." The antique dealer smiled and said, "Indeed; that's what makes it such a valuable watch."

DID YOU HEAR ABOUT...?

Ogden Nash, America's poet laureate of irreverent verse, spoke for the nay sayers when he wrote, "There are two kinds of people who blow through life like a breeze. And one kind is gossipers, and the other kind is gossipees (*I'm a Stranger Myself*, 1938)." A breeze, cold or hot, is a minor event, often not even noticed; in any case, not worth getting into a dither about.

But the Jewish attitude to gossip is worlds apart from Nash's indifference. Our first clue comes from the Hebrew language which has a particularly harsh expression for gossip, "*lashon hara;*" it means evil speech. That is a clear judgment about gossip, and in Jewish ethical comments, gossip is painted in the blackest colors. The Sages of the Talmud considered it the first of a triad of evils linking gossip, slander and libel in a single continuum. The same Sages instituted a closing meditation to a major prayer, recited three times daily, which ends with a moving personal appeal, "O Lord, guard my tongue from evil…" The "evil" meant by the prayer is evil speech. Where *lashon hara* is concerned, the Sages believed in the domino theory. They were certain that unchecked gossip, even if it begins in a mild low-key way, inevitably escalates to slander which in turn opens the flood-gates to libel. They saw it as a social cancer that has the power to destroy trust between people, leading ultimately to the collapse of society. They enlarged the meaning of the Torah's prohibition, "Keep far from falsehood" (Exodus 23:7) by declaring it a warning against every kind of gossip (Yalkut Shimoni 352). The Jerusalem Talmud regards gossip as the equivalent of the cardinal Jewish sins of apostasy, sexual perversion and murder. Even more, the transgressor forfeits both this world and the world to come (Peah, Ch.1). In general, the Sages did not shy away from extreme language in condemning *lashon hara*. "Says the Holy One, Blessed be He, 'This world is not large enough to accommodate both the teller of *lashon hara* and Me' (TB Arahin, 15a)." "The more evil the gossip, the further God is driven away from the universe (Midrash Dvarim Rabba, Ch.5)." "*Lashon hara* may be compared to spears and arrows that have a single aim, to kill a human being (Yalkut Shimoni, Mishlai 961)."

What is the fear that underlies these attitudes to gossip, and why such florid warnings about the consequences of loose tongues? Jewish religious belief looks upon every human being as possessing an inalienable right to his/her good name. Therefore, when we besmirch another person's good name, we are guilty of destroying part of that person's essence. Maimonides, the incomparable codifier of Talmudic jurisprudence, summarized the Jewish attitude to gossip, slander and libel in a brief passage, "Tale bearing consists of stories and telling them from one person to another. Even should the talebearer say, 'this is what I have heard from others,' and even though the stories are true, it is the equivalent of destroying the world. A far worse sin – a violation of a specific biblical prohibition – is to engage in evil gossip, intentionally demeaning another person, even though the report may be true (Mishna Torah, Day'ot, 7:2)."

It is worth noting that the Jewish mystical tradition deemed the faculty of speech to be the characteristic, par excellence, of human beings, differentiating us from all other creatures. In the mystical view, God was referring to the attribute of speech when He said, "Let us make man in Our image and in Our likeness (Genesis 1:26)." It is speech that makes us God-like, granting us a power which is both the most exalted and also the most dangerous.

Surprisingly there are fewer jokes about gossip in the collections of Jewish humor than what one might expect. Puzzling too is that the jokes found seem to lack the defining elements that would identify them as specifically Jewish. Often they appear to be derivative, absorbed from non-Jewish sources.

Our opening examples point to the persistence of gossip. They take for granted that gossip is as pervasive as the air we breathe. They also reflect the need for a higher standard of awareness.

In one respect, life in the Garden of Eden must have been exceptionally difficult for Adam and Eve. Poor souls, they had no one to gossip about.

―――

A man responded with great indignation to the accusation that he was a harmful gossip, "I do not indulge in gossip," he ve-

hemently declared. "What I tell people is not gossip, it is not slander, it is not libel; it's character analysis.

━━∿∿━━

Gossip confronts us with the problem of boundaries. Can we recognize the point where gossip ceases to be frivolous and crosses the line into destructive behavior? Since this is often not possible the issue of limits and boundaries never goes away. The Jewish view has always been that it is better to err on the side of avoidance than to risk the seductive allure and consequences of unregulated speech. Jewish ethics, as we have seen, relies heavily on the power of warning and admonition. Jewish teachers for at least two thousand years have lashed out at evil speech in vivid, extreme language.

That tradition has not changed. To the present day, Jewish moralistic texts do not hesitate to equate malicious gossip with murder. Some go further and declare that even a single act of *lashon hara* is a case of multiple murders. The three-fold victims are the gossiper, the passive listener, and the targeted victim. Such characterization is, of course, extreme hyperbole and is intended to describe the destruction of the victim's name and honor. The victim may never know how, why, and by whom. He knows only that somehow he has lost the trust and respect he once enjoyed. The evil gossiper dies in a different sense. His perverse pleasure in ruining the names of other people creates an ever-thickening layer of moral indifference around his own heart. The third victim is the listener who hears the gossip and does not protest it. He too suffers a kind of dying, the loss of moral sensitivity. His silence abets and stimulates socially loathsome conduct and contributes to an ever widening circle of evil.

MORE JOKES ABOUT THE EVILS OF GOSSIP

Two friends meet in the beauty parlor. While waiting for their turn, one comments to the other, "I've heard that Rosie has moved back to town. I'm dying to see her, to see if she still has that girlish figure that we used to envy." Her friend snickers and says, "Don't hold your breath. I've already seen her. I can tell you she still has her girlish figure and a lot more too."

⟨⟨∿∿⟩⟩

One gossip meets another and exclaims, "Can you believe it? I tell you, it's a scandal! Do you remember that sweet child, our friend Ada's daughter? She was always so affectionate, so devoted to her family." The second gossip replies, "Of course I remember her, and I can tell you her heart still belongs to her daddy. Unfortunately, she gives the rest of her body to a lot of other people."

⟨⟨∿∿⟩⟩

How can you tell the difference between gossip and news? It all depends on whether you are the teller or the listener.

⟨⟨∿∿⟩⟩

While his wife was out shopping, he remained at home. The phone rang. It was a friend of his wife wishing to speak to her. He said, "I'm sorry, she's not at home, but feel free to share any gossip with me. I'll be sure to pass it on to her."

⟨⟨∿∿⟩⟩

One Jew protests his innocence to another, "Don't blame me. I know how to keep a secret. It's those big mouth neighbors whom I confide in. They're the ones who don't know how to keep a secret."

⟨⟨∿∿⟩⟩

A gossipy woman remarked to her friend, "I don't mean to upset you, but I think you should know that there are rumors that your husband is having liaisons with young women." The friend responded coolly, "My husband is sixty-five years old. If he wants to chase after young women and make a fool of himself, let him. Haven't you ever seen dogs chasing after automobiles? Does that mean that they know how to drive?"

⎯⎯∧∧⎯⎯

Four friends met religiously once a week for lunch and an afternoon of cards. On one occasion, one of them blurted out a long-held secret to the others, "I have a confession to make, something I have to get off my chest. I'm a kleptomaniac. But please don't worry. You are the best friends I have in the whole world. I would never take anything that belongs to any of you." Hearing her confession, a second member of the group spoke up, "I too have something to confess. I'm a nymphomaniac, but please don't let this upset you. You are my dearest friends. I have never had an affair with your husbands, and I never will." A third member of the group felt impelled to make her own confession, "I'm a lesbian, but out of respect for each of you and for our friendship, I will never attempt to involve any of you sexually." At this, the fourth friend spoke up, "I too have a secret to confess. I'm a gossip, so please excuse me. I have an urgent call to make."

HOPE, THE HEARTBEAT OF THE JEW

Perhaps the supreme Jewish mystery in the face of persistent persecutions from ancient to modern times is that Judaism remains a religion of hope. Our oldest Jewish narratives, preserved in the Bible and experienced through many rituals, keep alive the memory of enslavements and exiles endured by our ancestors. Our religious calendar sets aside days and seasons to recall the destruction of our homeland and the loss of our national independence. In our prayers, we recite aloud tragic recollections of attacks upon our religious beliefs, recalling many points in our history when we were labeled a pariah people among the nations, and were made the scapegoats for the fury of other faiths and of secular powers. In recent memory we were targeted for extinction by the cruelest national ideology history has ever known. Today, religious extremism in several quarters of the world has revived the most hateful calumnies and vilifications against Jews and Judaism. In numbers and in misery, the toll among Jews has been mind numbing; small wonder that Jews have been called history's ever-dying people.

But if we are the keepers of a tragic record, we are also the bearers of an unbroken message of hope. We commemorate the story of our ancient enslavement in order to gain hope from their moment of redemption. When we mourn the loss of homeland, we also resolve to return and rebuild it. Incredibly, our four thousand year history is a never-ending tale of a people able to keep alive old hopes and to create new ones. Across many centuries and many landscapes Jews have found ways to regroup, to move on, and to rebuild. Hope has been the engine of our saga of physical and spiritual rebirth.

In the Egyptian National Museum in Cairo, there is a stele, a stone monument engraved with the boast of Mernepta, King of Egypt in the Fourteenth Century BCE proclaiming that "Israel is laid waste; its seed is no more." Mernepta's haughty words are the oldest attestation to the people of Israel outside the Bible. I once stood in front of that monument from the ancient past. I could almost visualize the gloating look on Mernepta's face as he proclaimed the death of the Israelites. His victory boast was in vain, as have been the boasts of other would-be destroyers of the Jewish people. Somehow we found deep wells of hope from which we drew the will and the faith to establish new centers of Jewish civilization. Remarkably, there is no doctrine of fatalism or of withdrawal from life in Judaism. Jews cling tenaciously to hope. In Jewish thinking, hope rises to the level of a dogma.

When did hope first appear as a manifestation of the Jewish spirit? It was born at the moment that Judaism entered history with its belief in the transformation of the world through the doctrine of monotheism. Judaism brought to the world the dream that humanity would be linked in a fellowship of shared faith; that the one transcendent God would bestow upon humanity the gift of world-wide tranquility. It is a dream that defies the realities of history.

Classical Judaism shares many beliefs with its daughter religions, Christianity and Islam, including the dream of a future redemption beyond this world. But Judaism, uniquely, never allowed itself to become an other-worldly religion. It never surrendered the world of the here and now. It has always taught that the work of redemption begins in this world through unremitting dedication to *"tikkun olam"* (the repairing of the world). In Jewish theological language, the Creator bequeathed to us a plan of perfection, but left in our hands an unfinished world. According to this teaching, we are more than just another species among countless others in the plan of creation. Ours is the highest calling, what Jewish tradition calls a partnership with God, charging us with the task of completing the work of creation. That God conceives of us as partners in the greatest of all ventures is the greatest of all compliments. It is the bottomless well of never-ending inspiration from which Jewish teaching draws its optimism.

Jewish humor lays a heavy hand on any sacred concept. Hope is no exception. It offers up a rich banquet for Jewish humor precisely because it is so often thwarted. Yet Jewish jokes mocking hope are generally subdued and tend not to evoke great laughter. Even when they deliver a sharp sting, they seem to display a grudging admiration for the poor souls who wallow in misfortune and defeat, but will not surrender hope. The jokes that tread heavily on optimism, when read correctly, give the lie to despair. They help us to recognize that Jews have always responded to an inner voice urging them to rise from the ashes and to recreate themselves.

We examine two stories to illustrate how Jews would not surrender hope even in the most adverse circumstances.

> *The Gentile nobleman, known as the Graf, was owner and sovereign of the town and its surrounding land. He found himself perplexed by the strange antics of the town's poorest Jew. He watched him measure off a few paces, stop and enter some calculations in a tattered note-book. The Graf's bemusement grew as the Jew repeated the process over and over again. Finally, unable to contain his curiosity, he called out, "Jew, what exactly are you trying to figure out?" The poor man replied, "Your Excellency, I am trying to calculate how much I would have to pay you to acquire this town from you." The Graf exploded in raucous laughter. "Fool," he said, "Don't you realize that this town would cost you a great fortune, and you don't have even a penny to your name?" The Jew responded, "Sir Graf, that is today, but who can predict what tomorrow may bring?"*

⚡⚡⚡

> *A peddler depended for his livelihood on a rickety wagon and an old horse. The peddler found himself in a terrible predicament. The cost of feeding the horse took away almost everything he earned. One day, a novel solution leaped into his mind. He would train the horse to get along without food. The next day the experiment began. That morning he cut the horse's rations in half. It seemed to make no difference to the horse. For an entire week, eating half his usual amount of oats, the horse plodded along as always. The peddler was elated. At the start of the second week, encouraged by his success, he again reduced the rations by half, and again the horse continued to pull the wagon. The peddler could barely contain his joy as he saw his earnings grow. Emboldened by his brilliant plan, he added a new wrinkle. One day each week, he gave the horse nothing to eat. Dutifully, the horse continued to pull the*

wagon. After several weeks more, the peddler added a second day of fasting to the weekly routine, and then a third day and a fourth, until finally the horse was being fed only one day a week. Who can imagine the peddler's exultation when he was finally ready to begin the ultimate test? That week he gave the horse nothing. True, the horse pulled the wagon more slowly, but now every penny received was total profit. The next day disaster struck. The horse stopped in his tracks, shuddered, and fell dead. The peddler, unnerved and uncomprehending, came down from his perch on the wagon, heaved an anguished sigh, and rebuked the dead animal, "Ungrateful beast; now that I finally had you trained, look what you've done to me!"

⸺⹀⹀⹀⸺

The two stories are variations on the theme of hope in the face of an implacable reality. The story of the Graf and the penniless Jew evokes memories of the Eastern European landscape of earlier centuries. There were two social classes, a heritage from medieval times. One was made up of gentile families who held title to vast expanses of land. They were its true rulers in every sense. They amassed their fortunes from the rents and taxes they collected from the peasant class, non-Jews and Jews alike. Great numbers of Jews lived in the villages of these fiefdoms, perpetually in debt to the Grafs who owned the land. A Graf might be cruel or kindly disposed towards his vassals. He might be hateful to his Jews or think of them as useful contributors to his wealth. However he chose to present himself, he and his peasants knew that he was absolute ruler. What then could be more unimaginable, more clownish, than the Jew's ungrounded notion that a day might come when their positions would be reversed?

But this is the fundamental characteristic of hope. It imagines life radically transformed. Hope connects to life and to the future through a mental trick. It lives in a world of "as if." Jews have always played this mind game and have institutionalized it in the experience of the weekly Sabbath. It is a day of total change, of rest from struggle; a day when money, the supreme symbol of competition and separation, is put aside; a day dedicated to togetherness and peace. This island of time is the extreme expression of the power of hope and a belief in a time when every day will be lived as a Sabbath.

Even more than the first story, the peddler tale portrays the bleak and wretched life of Jews who awakened each day to face the same struggle. Cutting corners for them was not an option; it was a given. The slow clip-clop of the famished horse, barely able to pull the wagon, is a metaphor for a people mired in an unequal struggle for physical and spiritual survival. The peddler needs no coaching to know that what passes for today's good fortune can be undone by tomorrow's misfortunes. Yet it's not a despairing story. The peddler is the image of the Jewish people. We can be confident that for him giving up is not an option.

When we look closely at the people who personify hope in these two tales we see that they are not paralyzed by their circumstances. Adverse fortune does not turn them into robots. They are not distracted from their goal by the detours or obstacles along the road, and failures do not defeat them. They are activists who never stop trying; they do not give up their search for new ways to improve their lives. Tomorrow is not an illusion for them; it is a work in progress. The characters in these jokes live among people whose lives are similarly deprived. They know that the world they dream of will not come about in a sudden flash. It will come in stages as more and more people find seats at the table of a better life. When we bind ourselves to high ethical standards, we commit ourselves both to the present and to the future. We make hope tangible by how we lead our own lives and by the example we provide for others.

MORE STORIES ABOUT HOPE

A Jew wrote a letter to his friend, "You know that I have tried one business after another and that none of them has succeeded. I have now started a new one, and this time I have absolute confidence that I will have a great success. I have opened up a store the likes of which no one has seen before. It is truly unique; it cannot miss. On one side of the store I shall sell bread, and on the other side I shall sell burial shrouds. In this way, everyone, both the living and the dead, will need my merchandise." A few months passed. The friend received a second letter, "Alas, the store is closed. What can I tell you? The people in this town are neither alive nor dead."

—∽∽∿∾—

A boat laden with a cargo of wine was attacked by a huge whale. The beast rammed the boat repeatedly and tossed it every which way. The captain of the vessel feared that the boat might capsize. He ordered the crew to cast overboard the entire cargo. The cartons broke apart in the water and many bottles ended up in the belly of the whale. During the attack, a number of passengers, a Jew among them, were swept over the side and swallowed by the whale. The story has entered the annals of the legends of the sea because of its strange ending. Some time after the attack on the boat, the body of a huge sea creature was washed ashore. Fishermen rushed to the carcass and began to cut it open. Inside its belly they found a Jew selling wine to his fellow passengers.

—∽∽∿∾—

On a Shabbat afternoon, two Jews met while out for a stroll. One was a builder of houses, the other an indigent scholar. He was filled with curiosity about his companion's path to riches. The builder explained, "My first venture was a failure. I put into it everything I had inherited from my father, and I lost it all." The scholar asked, "In that case, how were you able to get back on your feet again?" He replied, "I did what all builders do. I made a successful bid on an even larger project. With the down payment I received, I was able to satisfy some of my creditors. I used the rest to purchase new buildings materials." Impressed by his friend's skill at reviving his career, the scholar had another question, "Is this what accounts for your great wealth today?" The builder looked at him and said, "Not at all. As bad as my first experience was, the second one was worse. Again I lost everything. And again I used the same strategy. I made a successful bid and got an even larger contract. I satisfied some of my creditors with the down payment, and with what was left I bought new building supplies." The scholar interrupted him, "Surely then, this is how you became wealthy. "Oh no," came the reply. "This one too was a colossal failure, bigger than the other ones combined." Completely befuddled, the scholar managed one last question, "But if that's the case, where does it all end?" The builder breathed deeply and answered, "Where does it end? It ends the way everything ends. It ends when I die."

—————

Among the poor, Motke took second place to no one. He was the poorest of them all. It wasn't for lack of trying. Motke had tried many things, but no matter what he turned to, he failed. Even as a beggar he had no success. But Motke was not to be pitied. He was rich in one talent. Not a year passed without his wife bearing a new addition to their brood. No one could understand how Motke was able to retain his optimism. Surely no one was as burdened under the yoke of poverty as much as Motke. Friends and even strangers would ask him, "Motke, with so many little ones to raise, what will happen to them when they grow up, how will they support themselves?" Motke would politely consider the question, and to each one he would reply, "I do not worry about the future. My children, may they all be well, will not lack for opportunities. They will be like all Jewish children. Some of them will become builders, some will become tutors of little children, some will become store keepers, and some may even end up as beggars. No matter what path they will choose, they will know what it means to have failures. I have nothing material to give to them, but I do have one gift I can give to them. I shall tell them that if God wills it, they will succeed."

WHERE JEWS ARE FOOLS AND FOOLS ARE JEWS

What does a town have to do to earn fame as a place of fools? Helm, in Eastern Poland, was such a town. Merely mentioning its name to Jews can evoke smiles and even laughter. The term, "*Helemer naronim*" - Helmite fools – was a familiar expression. In a sense, Helm is a part of my identity. I come from Helm stock. My maternal grandfather, an immensely learned Rabbi and his extended family were born in Helm. My grandfather was in every way the antithesis of what Jewish story-telling associates with Helm. On one occasion, we talked about the origin of the town's name. I suggested that it might relate to "*holem*" - a dream. Some dreams, no matter how surrealistic or fantastic, seem entirely plausible in the dream state. It is only on awakening that they reveal themselves as utterly absurd. Helm, I said, shares that quality with dreams. Perhaps this might explain Helm stories that seem plausible in the telling, but which on reflection are utterly improbable. My grandfather proposed his own explanation. "Someone must have hated some Jews in Helm and invented those stories to make fun of them."

Jewish story-telling handed down its own myth to explain how Helm became the capitol city of Jewish fools. Helm, it tells us, traces back to the earliest moments of creation when the world was largely empty of human beings. God selected a heavenly angel for a mission of greatest importance, entrusting to him a large sack filled with the souls of unborn fools. God instructed the angel to scatter the souls throughout the world. The angel set out on his journey, but during the descent from heaven disaster struck. The sack opened, spilling the souls in a single place, in a remote corner of Poland. As time passed, a Jewish community grew up in that place. Mysteriously – so at first it seemed – all of their children were born with the souls of fools, and it has continued this way throughout the generations. Thus the legacy of Helm was established, and so it has remained.

Many of the tales set in Helm invite comparison with the legends of fools known from other folk literatures. Let it be said that Helm's Jewish fools need not take a back seat to the fools of any other group. Like fools everywhere, they are never cognizant that they are fools. Their distinction is that they are determinedly loyal to the sanctified ways of Jewish tradition. They employ tutors to teach their children the ways of Torah. They are a caring community. They scrupulously place charity in their synagogue's collection box. They share equitably all burdens that may beset their community. In Helm, collaborative thinking is the preferred way of dealing with any issue. With ponderous solemnity and endless patience, without ever rushing to judgment, the rabbi of Helm and the esteemed council of elders meet to discuss and settle all issues. No problem, large or small, is ever left unresolved.

But Helm, after all, is a town of fools. A Helm solution, no matter how ingenious, is always ludicrous. With impeccable logic and with an astonishing ability to dice all issues into a thousand tiny pieces, Helm's leaders contrive solutions that make no sense at all – except to the Jews of Helm.

We laugh at the Jews of Helm. But strangely, even as we laugh at their antics, Helm's Jews command our admiration. They have mastered the art of living as a genuine community where everyone works for the benefit of everyone else. There is no selfishness in Helm. Arrogance is nowhere to be found. Helm's Jews are not boastful. They do not gossip, nor do they waste precious hours practicing deceit. No problem in Helm is left unacknowledged or allowed to fester. The Jews of Helm possessed an intuitive understanding that no good ever comes from leaping to an instant solution to a problem. A rash decision is unthinkable in Helm. Long-winded, unhurried discussion is the only way to arrive at the best solution, and in Helm a solution is always found. We won't be wrong if we look upon Helm jokes as the Jewish salute to the goodness latent in each of us.

The selection of Helm humor highlights one of the unique talents of its Jews, their prodigious powers of clear-headed, logical thinking. Without this quality, Helm would simply not be Helm.

Jews of Helm cared greatly about each other's woes. There was great empathy among them. One person's misfortune quickly became someone else's misery. As a result, every Helm Jew was a non-stop worrier. At times their worries were so overwhelming that the rabbi became concerned lest it lead to mass depression. He devised a plan which was as brilliant as it was simple, and presented it to the council of elders. After a full week of discussion and debate, the elders gave the plan their unanimous endorsement. The rabbi announced to the entire community the appointment of Zalman Itzik the candle-maker, revered by all the Jews of Helm, who would henceforth serve as the town's official worrier. Zalman Itzik was to be paid a salary that exceeded his earnings as a candle-maker. The plan was greeted with great enthusiasm throughout the community, but met with unexpected failure. Zalman Itzik was overheard boasting to his wife, Yenta Sora, that with his new salary they would never have to worry again.

—∾∿∾—

Helm was situated on both banks of a river. An old, narrow bridge provided the sole access from one side to the other. The bridge had become dangerous because of a large hole that had developed in its center. A number of serious accidents had already occurred when unwary pedestrians had fallen through the hole and suffered grievous injuries. The council of elders and the rabbi met to consider various ways to prevent further misfortunes and even, God forbid, the possibility that people might actually fall to their deaths. The rabbi admonished the elders to spare no effort to devise the best plan. After a week of non-stop day and night meetings, a unanimous decision was reached to build a hospital at the side of the bridge.

—∾∿∾—

Helm stories serve as a litmus test for the validity of the basic thesis that Jewish jokes can be pointers to ethical goals. The Jews of Helm are, without question, artless, naïve and foolish. They are also irrepressibly good. Despite their foolishness, they succeed in fashioning a loving community, free of vulgarity and egotistical display. No one in Helm competes to diminish the sanctity of another person. Everyone in Helm instinctively understands that the human mind is an incomparable blessing, a miraculous gift that is best appreciated when placed at the service of others.

Abraham Joshua Heschel, the revered Jewish theologian and social activist of the last century, taught that a sense of wonder is at the
heart of the spiritual life. The Jews of Helm took no courses in ethics
or in moral philosophy, but they possessed a sense of wonder to an
uncommon degree. They marveled at everything in nature; they
marveled too at fellow human beings. They also possessed other in-
gredients of a spiritual life. There was no rancor in their speech, no
competition for status. They worried constantly about the have-nots
in their community, and acted to find solutions to their problems.
Their synagogue was both a center of fervent prayer and a center of
outreach to everyone in need. Rather than be self-absorbed, they
chose a life saturated with sympathy and empathy. Helm jokes can
be read as the antics of simpletons, but they can also prod us to think
about ethical qualities that are often missing from our personal lives
and our communities. Judged by these criteria, Helm's fools have
much to teach us.

MORE JOKES ABOUT THE FOOLS OF HELM

*Helm was gripped by an emergency. Thieves had entered the
town one night and had ransacked several houses. To allay the
fears of the townspeople the rabbi and the council of elders met
without delay to ponder what could be done to punish any future violators of the law. After long discussion lasting many
days, they reached a decision. They issued the following proclamation to all the citizens of the town, "Be it known to all Jews
of Helm and to all others who shall enter our town, that any
thief who shall be apprehended shall be brought without delay
to the community hall. Two holes shall be drilled into one of the
walls. The thief shall be made to face the wall and place his
arms into the holes. On the other side of the wall, he shall be
made to tightly grasp a metal rod with his two hands. In this
way, we shall prevent him from withdrawing his arms from
the holes and escaping."*

As the generations passed, Helm's population grew larger. In time the cemetery was no longer adequate. Helm's rabbi summoned the council of elders to devise a plan to solve the problem. For seven days and seven nights they sat together, taking time off only for the Sabbath. Many possible solutions were heard and discussed, and each one was examined in minutest detail for its advantages and disadvantages. At last the elders gave their unanimous support to the proposal that additional land be acquired adjacent to the existing cemetery. They also devised a plan to determine how much land would be needed. On the next Sabbath a proclamation was read aloud in the synagogue to all of Helm's Jews, "Fellow Jews of Helm, be advised that tomorrow all Jews of our community, the elderly and the not elderly, men, women and children, without exception, are to gather in the field adjacent to the cemetery. They are to lie down side-by-side, row by row. In that way we shall determine precisely how much new burial land we shall need to meet our needs."

⸜⸝⸜⸝

A group of Helm's wisest citizens sat engrossed in an important medical issue, "Are the doctors correct when they say that smoking is injurious to health? If they are right, we shall have to take steps to protect the lives of the Jews of Helm." One of the group expressed his firm opinion, "The physicians are always trying to frighten us. It is not true that smoking is harmful. My father smoked all his life and he lived to ninety." A second person agreed, "Smoking has nothing to do with health. I had a baby brother. He never once touched a cigarette, and he died at the age of two.

⸜⸝⸜⸝

A Helm housewife went to the market to purchase a herring and a loaf of bread. "How much are they," she asked. "Fourteen kopeks," she was told. "Fourteen kopeks for a herring and bread," she replied in astonishment. Concerned that the merchant was asking an unfair price, she said, "I think you made a mistake. It should be eleven kopeks." The merchant replied, "No way; the bread is seven kopeks and the herring is seven kopeks. That comes to fourteen." The woman persisted and said, "The way I calculate, seven plus seven equal eleven, not fourteen." The merchant was amazed by her arithmetic, "What kind of strange calculation are you using? Seven and seven are always fourteen." Again the customer persisted. "Let me show you why it's eleven. I have four children from my first husband. After his death, I married a widower. He too had four children from his first marriage. He and I have been blessed with three additional children. That means that I'm the mother of seven children and he is the father of seven children, but between us there are eleven children. Seven and seven equal eleven."

〜〜〜〜

Thieves entered <u>Helm</u> one night and made off with the synagogue's charity box. Great anguish spread through the town at the thought that someone could have perpetrated such a vile, immoral act. The rabbi did not waste a moment. He summoned the council of elders to deliberate the matter and to take steps to assure that the poor would never again have their rights to charity violated. After many days and nights of protracted deliberation, the elders summoned the community and announced their decision, "A new charity box will be purchased and the needs of the poor will be protected. To prevent a recurrence of the theft, the new charity box will be suspended from the synagogue's ceiling out of the reach of thieves. The Jews of <u>Helm</u> rejoiced at the wisdom of their leaders. Unfortunately, an unexpected problem arose soon after the new charity box was installed. True, no thief could reach it and make off with its contents, but it was now also out of the reach of Jews who wished to add coins to the box, and worst of all, the poor could not reach it either. Again the rabbi acted quickly and decisively. He reconvened the council of elders, and after long and vigor-

ous discussion they solved the problem to everyone's satisfaction. They decreed that the charity box was to remain suspended high above the floor to discourage thieves, and they further decreed that a tall ladder would be placed beneath the charity box so that both contributors and the poor would be able to reach it without difficulty.

~~~

The Jews of Helm beheld everything in nature as a gift from God. One warm summer day, two Jews of Helm reclined in a grassy field, marveling at how the wonders about them testify to the matchless wisdom of the Creator. In a nearby meadow, a cow was munching on the grass, while overhead a song bird was chirping a sweet melody as it flew in lazy circles above the meadow. One Jew asked the other, "Why is it that the Creator gave wings to the birds, but not to the cows?" Just as the other Jew opened his mouth to answer, the songbird swooped low and let fall a splattering which landed on his head. His companion watched him wipe himself clean and said, "Never mind, I think I have just received an answer to my question."

~~~

Helm's population had grown large. The synagogue could no longer accommodate all the Jews. A plan was announced to enlarge the building. A large number of men volunteered to climb the nearby mountain where a forest of large trees stood at the top. They felled many of the trees and turned them into logs. With great effort they lifted the logs to their shoulders and carried them down the mountain. A stranger passing by was astonished to see what the workers were doing. He advised them that it would be much easier, as well as quicker, if they would simply roll the logs down the mountain. The men of Helm immediately grasped the wisdom of his counsel. They carried all the logs back up to the top of the mountain and rolled them down.

⎯⌇⌇⌇⎯

It had been a harsh winter, one of the cruelest that anyone
could remember. As the bitter months of cold were at last near-
ing their end, Helm's most famous sage was observed sitting
alone in his home, silent and brooding. His friends, out of concern for him, tried to find out the source of his sadness. He said
to them, "I am upset because our wise rabbis of old made a terrible error when they arranged our calendar. They ordained
that in a Jewish leap year we must have two months of Adar
while it is still winter. Had I been among them, I would have
protested the terrible harm they have caused to every Jew in
every generation. I would have said to them, "Honored rabbis,
let the doubled month be observed in the summer, in the month
of Tammuz, the hottest month of the year, when we don't need
boots because of the snow, and when we don't have to chop
down trees to heat our homes."

⎯⌇⌇⌇⎯

A Jew of Helm sought out the rabbi for advice on how to solve
a problem that had long been vexing him. "Rabbi," he asked,
"Which is more important, the sun or the moon?" The rabbi
pondered for several minutes, examining the question from
every angle. After much cogitation, he carefully expressed his
opinion, "The moon is more important than the sun. The moon
shines at night when we need the light, whereas the sun shines
in the daytime when we really don't need it.

⎯⌇⌇⌇⎯

It was a balmy, cloudless day in Helm, and Avrum was enjoying his afternoon walk. Soon he met up with Yossel who
was also out for a stroll. Avrum thought it odd that Yossel was
carrying an umbrella on such a beautiful day. As they walked
along, enjoying the beauty of the day and engrossed in deep

conversation, neither of them noticed that the sky had darkened until suddenly a torrential downpour began to fall. Yossel paid no attention to the rain and did not bother to open the umbrella. Avrum shouted to him, "Yossel, you brought the umbrella. It will give us some protection. Open it!" Yossel replied, "It won't do us any good. It's all full of holes." Avrum asked, "Why then did you bring it?" Yossel answered, "I didn't think it would rain."

AFTERTHOUGHT:
THE SAD FACE OF JEWISH HUMOR

⚡〰〰⚡

Over and over in our study we have come across jokes that are simply unhappy tales that climax with mean put-downs, and yet they have the power to make us laugh. I have a special name for this kind of laughter. I call it the "pratfall response," a term I have taken from a routine featured in old time burlesque. Comedians would enact a mock chase. At the moment when the victim was about to be caught, he would throw a banana peel under the feet of his pursuer who promptly lost his footing and fell on his buttocks. That was the pratfall moment, and it never failed to convulse the audience in laughter. It was the laughter of seeing humor in another person's misfortune. What compels us to laugh at someone else's expense? Perhaps it is to congratulate ourselves that someone other than our selves was the victim.

Jewish history is studded with sad, painful events, so it is not surprising that many Jewish jokes connect to Jewish misfortunes. Even the Holocaust gave birth to a kind of Jewish black humor. Many people have come to regard the Jewish past as one long vale of tears. The historian, Salo Baron, considered this a distortion and labeled it "the lachrymose conception of Jewish history." This outlook fails to account for the spiritual and ethical joy that has always characterized the Jewish view of life. A true reading of Jewish life through the ages presents a balanced portrait in which the sad and the joyful receive their proper due. I have tried to be responsive to this balance by showing how even sad and embittered humor can connect us to the joy and blessedness that are our gift when we integrate Jewish ethical teachings into our lives.

GLOSSARY

~~~~

Texts Cited

BT – Babylonian Talmud, fifth century CE; compendium and discussions of Jewish religious law and folk-lore transmitted orally during previous centuries.

Dead Sea Scrolls – ancient Jewish manuscripts discovered in Israel in 1947, containing beliefs and practices of Jewish sectarian groups circa 200 BCE.

Hallel – chapters 113-118 of the Book of Psalms added to morning prayers on festival occasions.

JT – Jerusalem Talmud (more correctly, Talmud of Palestine), compendium and discussion of Jewish religious law and folk-lore, though less of the latter than in the Babylonian Talmud; completed about one hundred years earlier than BT; considered less authoritative than BT.

Kabbalah – a body of writings consisting of mystical interpretations of Torah and practices of Judaism.

Midrash - the collected rabbinic interpretations of narrative and legal biblical texts.

Mishnah – codex of oral legal traditions derived from Torah; published in the land of Israel, circa 200CE.

Mishneh Torah – Maimonides' restatement of Biblical and Talmudic laws and practices.

Torah –Five Books of Moses, from the Hebrew root meaning "teaching;" also commonly used to refer to the entirety of Hebrew Scripture.

Hebrew and Yiddish Terms and Names

Unless identified by the word Yiddish in parentheses, it can be assumed that the terms originate in Hebrew.

Badhan – a comic entertainer featured at festive gatherings : often through original rhymed humor.

Dorf – (Yiddish) - village, hamlet.

Dorf's Yid – (Yiddish) – small town Jew; often a pejorative, a "hick."

Ferd – (Yiddish) - horse, in slang an ignoramus, a fool

Gneyvat da'at – willful misrepresentation, deception, fraud; literally, "stealing someone's knowledge

Graf – (Yiddish) - a hereditary aristocrat, owner of vast tracts of land and villages; in pre-modern times, he controlled the destiny of those who lived on his land.

Hahnassat orhim – the act of extending hospitality to strangers, especially to the poor.

Hazan – chanter of public prayers; more recently the role evolved into a professional member of the clergy.

Hassid – a follower of the religious movement which popularized Jewish mystical teachings and customs. Its beginning was in 18th century as grass-roots revivalism.

Hannukah – an eight–day winter festival commemorating over-throw of tyrannical Syrian occupation of land of Israel in 165 BCE.

Kiddush – a prayer ceremony celebrating Sabbath and Biblically commanded festivals.

Kara'ism –a Jewish sect that observed only those commandments written in the Torah, without rabbinic elaborations and interpreta-tions. A follower of Kara'ism was called Kara'ite.

Maimonides – (1135 – 1204) towering genius, codifier and analyzer of entire corpus of Talmudic jurisprudence. He synthesized Jewish religious principles and Aristotelian philosophy.

Mohel – a religious functionary with authority to perform the ritual of circumcision on Jewish males

Melamed - teacher, tutor, but most often designation for instructor of young children in religious texts.

Mitnaged – a Jew opposed to Hassidic practices. (Plural, Mitnagdim – also the name of the anti Hassidic movement).

Mikveh – a pool of water drawn from naturally flowing sources, used for   immersion in purification rituals.

Nesheh – literally, a "bite." The Biblical term for forbidden interest charges on monetary loans, but permitted by rabbinic law when the loan is for commercial purposes.

Purim – a one day festival commemorating the victory of Persian Jews against the arch-oppressor Haman.

Pesah – Passover festival celebrating the redemption of the Hebrews from ancient Egyptian slavery.

Pidyon – in Hassidic practice, a voluntary monetary gift given to the Rebbe as a token of appreciation for his intervention, through prayer and sometimes magic, in a time of critical need.

Rashi – French Rabbi (1040–1105), writer of classical commentaries par excellence of the Bible and Talmud.

Rebbe –a popular designation for a Hassidic Rabbi; from Aramaic, meaning teacher.

Rosh Hashanah – a holiday marking the start of the Jewish year and the season of penitence.

Schnnorer – (Yiddish) a beggar; usually one who travels from town to town in search of alms.

Shabbat – Hebrew for Sabbath, observed as day of rest interrupting ordinary week-day routines.

Shadhan – arranger of marriages for a fee; the oldest equivalent of a Jewish dating service.

Shammes – the jack-of-all-trades master of all aspects of public prayer; almost always a lay person, adept at leading worship services and managing every ritual observance

Sheleg – snow; In Yiddish, "shnay."

Shalom Bayit –a tranquil household.

Shpiel – (Yiddish) a humorous presentation, akin to a comic monologue; usually a parody, often presented at festive religious celebrations.

Shohet – Rabbinically accredited slaughterer of cattle and poultry in accordance with Jewish dietary rules.

Shtetl – (Yiddish), village or town; usually larger than a dorf.

Sim̲hat Torah –the holiday that marks the completion and new beginning of the public reading of the Torah in the synagogue. It closes the series of fall holidays that begins with Rosh Hashanah. Literally it means, "Rejoicing of the Torah."

Sofayr – Scribe, writer of Torah scrolls and other religious documents, all of which must be written by hand.

Tam̲ha –Talmudic term for bitter herb used during Pesa̲h Seder ceremony, symbolizing the bitterness of slavery in Egypt.

Tzaddik – Literally a righteous person, but used by many H̲assidim as title for their Rabbi.

Tzedakah –Literally, an act of righteousness, but popularly a charitable gift, not limited to money.

Vilna – The Yiddish name for Vilnius, capitol city of Lithuania; famed for institutions of higher Jewish learning and as a center of secular Jewish culture; often referred to as the "Jerusalem of Lithuania."

Yetzer Harah – The impulse to do evil;

Yetzer Tov – The impulse to do good,

Yiddish – The language of Eastern European Jewry, descended from the German of the Middle Ages with copious additions of Hebrew and Slavic words.

RESOURCES

⟶∿∿⟵

First and foremost among the works from which I have bene-
fited is A. Droyanov's Hebrew trilogy, *"Sefer Habedi̱ha V'ha̱hidud."* It
is by far our greatest anthology of Jewish humor (Dvir Publishers,
Tel Aviv, 1939).

"A Treasury of Jewish Folklore" by Nathan Ausubel was my first
introduction to the immensity of Jewish humor. I continue to consult
it (Crown Publishers, N.Y., 1948).

I found much useful material in Henry Spalding's *"Encyclopedia
of Jewish Humor"* (Jonathan David Publishers, N.Y., 1969).

Of more recent works, Joseph Telushkin's *"Jewish Humor – What
the Best Jewish Jokes Say about the Jews"* is deservedly popular. It is
largely about how Jews have responded to critical changes in Jewish
life patterns in recent history (William Morrow & Co., N.Y., 1992).

B.J. Bialosotzky's excellent Yiddish volume on Jewish humor,
Yiddisher Humor Un Yiddishe Laytzim" (*Jewish Humor and Jewish
Jesters*) is short on jokes, but long and edifying on commentary. He
adroitly uses well-known jokes as introductions to rewarding essays on the many faces of Jewish character. (Cyco Publishers, N.Y.,
1963).

Two new works in Hebrew by Adir Cohen have added much to
my knowledge. His *"Sefer Hahumor Hayehudi Hagadol"* (*The Big Book
of Jewish Humor*) is a large scale anthology of jokes arranged according to many categories. It provides no commentary other than
an introductory chapter (Kinneret, Zimora-Bitan, Dvir Publishers,
Or Yehuda, Israel, 2004). His other volume, *"Hahumor Shel Am Yis-
rael Ledorotav"* (*Jewish Humor Through the Ages*), is a wide-ranging
work whose special contribution is the author's analysis of contem-

porary areas of Jewish humor in Israel and America. It features such topics and types as the Jewish-American Princess, and the humor of Lenny Bruce and Woody Allen (Amatzia Publishers, Haifa, 2004).

Ruth Wisse's essay "Some Serious Thoughts About Jewish Humor" (Leo Baeck Institute, New York/Berlin, 2001) is a splendid examination of how Jewish humor releases the many tensions that Jews encounter with their separate existence and in their relations with the surrounding society. Her approach does not include a relationship between Jewish humor and Jewish ethical values.

Many works have been helpful regarding ethics in the Jewish tradition. Haim Cohen's "Human Rights in Jewish Law" proved especially beneficial (Ktav, N.Y., 1984).

Mena_hem Alon's multi-volume Hebrew opus, "Hamishpat Ha'ivri" ("Jewish Jurisprudence") was an excellent source for tracing historic developments of important Jewish ethical concepts (The Magnes Press-Hebrew University, Jerusalem, 1973).

As always, comprehensive articles on many ethical themes in Encyclopedia Judaica were a source of important insights (Keter Publishers, Jerusalem 1972).

Two volumes of Edmond Kahn's essays provided much general information about how American law deals with injustice and with moral dilemmas: "The Moral Decision" (Indiana University Press, 1955) and "Confronting Injustice" (Little, Brown, Boston, 1962).

IN APPRECIATION

Among the anthologists who have preserved the oral treasury of Jewish humor, pride of place belongs to a man unknown to English readers. Alter Droyanov stands at the head of all who labored in the vast field of Jewish humor during the past one hundred years. Born in 1870 in Vilna, Lithuania he was one of the circle of writers who gravitated to the poet Hayyim Nahman Bialik in Odessa, Russia. With Bialik he settled in Tel Aviv in 1921. There he became an executive and editor of the Hebrew publishing house, Dvir. His magnum opus, *Sefer Habediha Vehahidud* (*The Book of Jewish Wit and Humor*) was completed in 1939. In three volumes he assembled more than three thousand examples of Jewish humor grouped under thirty five different headings, drawn mainly from Eastern European Yiddish sources.

His work appeared just as the ominous black cloud of Nazism was poised to unleash a torrent of death and destruction upon the European Jewish centers that had given birth to that vast oral heritage. Droyanov's labors, perhaps unintended, were an act of rescue that saved the heritage of Jewish humor from the ravages that were soon to obliterate so much Jewish creativity. We can only be grateful that he left us an intact body of authentic Jewish folk-lore, one that opens many windows into the Jewish soul. Contemporary collectors of Jewish humor are often unaware that significant parts of their repertoire have antecedents in Droyanov's magisterial collection. I acknowledge my personal debt to Droyanov. Substantial portions of the material in this book are my renderings into English of his translations of jokes and anecdotes from Yiddish into Hebrew. They are reminders of how much we remain obligated to him.

Droyanov did not attempt to interpret the stories in his collection. He believed that Jewish humor was a late arrival on the stage of Jewish history, and that it owes its immense vitality to the explosive growth of secular Jewish forces in the late nineteenth and early twentieth centuries. He believed that rabbinic tradition, from earliest times, suppressed humor among Jews. He cites sages of the Talmud and later Jewish moralists who heaped scorn upon tellers of jokes, fearing that jokes and jesting would degrade both public and personal morals. According to Droyanov, this accounts for the paucity of jokes and other forms of humor in Jewish writings prior to the eighteenth century. From my perspective, Droyanov's analysis is overly narrow. In earlier centuries, books published by Jews were overwhelmingly devoted to religious themes and far outnumbered the slender output of secular writings. The absence of humor in Jewish writings is testimony to the power of rabbinic influence in earlier times to suppress humor in print. It does not necessarily imply that there was not a continuous and rich tradition of orally transmitted humor.

As far back as the late Middle Ages, Jews staged elaborate, even bawdy Purim *spiels,* holiday spoofs that relied heavily on humor. We know also of the equally old tradition of the *bad̲h̲an,* the rhyming jester, who was a beloved figure at Jewish wedding celebrations. It is difficult to imagine the existence of such highly developed forms of humor in the absence of a supporting folk culture. Jokes, as a form of social commentary, did expand into a major facet of Jewish folk life under the influence of a growing Jewish secular culture, but they surely have a much longer history as a continuous evocation of the Jewish creative genius.

ACKNOWLEDGMENTS

I owe much to the adult students in the Cleveland Midrasha (formerly the Lehrhaus) who responded with lively give and take to a course I offered on Jewish humor. Their reactions led to the desire to fashion this study along the lines it has taken.

A number of family members and friends responded positively to my notion that many Jewish jokes are best understood as folk elaborations – even commentaries – on Jewish spiritual teachings. My children, Amy, Michael, Abby and Brenda, accepted uncritically my fatherly command to be critical readers of the manuscript as it proceeded through several trial evolutions. Their comments and suggestions were pure na_has for me and encouraged me to see the work through to completion.

Rabbi A. Nathan Abramowitz, Rabbi Moshe Adler, Joshua Glatzer, Professor Stevan Hopfoll, Rabbi Harold Kushner and Rabbi Jack Riemer gave careful feedback to major portions of the manuscript which they graciously read. I thank them for their encouragement.

Sadly, two precious friends, connoisseurs of humor, who enriched me over the years, have passed away. Dr. Robert Werman, physician, teacher, poet and friend for fifty years, used the internet to share his love of Jewish humor during his last years. Charles (Chuck) Elinsky never tired of trying out jokes on me from his seemingly endless stock. Through humor he brought grace to his last years despite the heavy burden of multiple illnesses.

Lifsa, my wife and best critic, is as shrewd an analyst of humor as anyone I have known. A simple lift of a quizzical eyebrow is her signal to me that a joke is not as funny as I thought it was. Sharing humor with her, especially the Jewish variety is one of the delights of our years together. This book is dedicated to her.